A
MASSIVE
SWELLING

D0028931

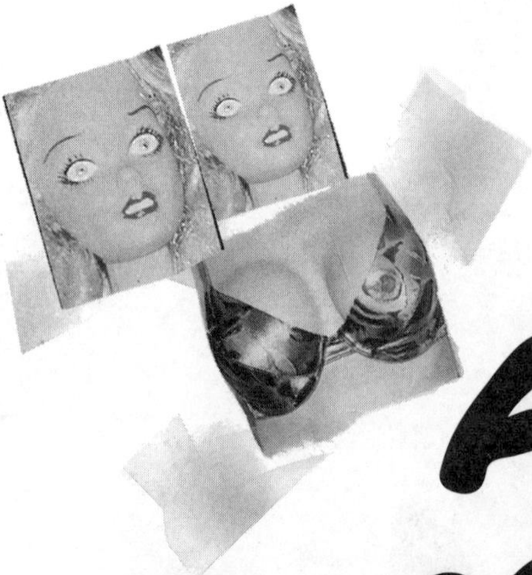

A MASSIVE SWEL

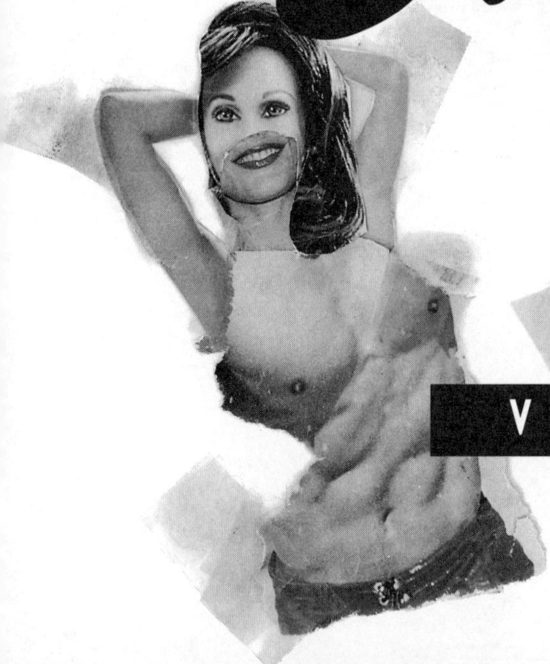

Viking

CINTRA WILSON

LING

Celebrity Re-examined
as a Grotesque,
Crippling Disease
and Other Cultural
Revelations

VIKING
Published by the Penguin Group
Penguin Putnam Inc., 375 Hudson Street,
New York, New York 10014, U.S.A.
Penguin Books Ltd, 27 Wrights Lane,
London W8 5TZ, England
Penguin Books Australia Ltd, Ringwood,
Victoria, Australia
Penguin Books Canada Ltd, 10 Alcorn Avenue,
Toronto, Ontario, Canada M4V 3B2
Penguin Books (N.Z.) Ltd, 182–190 Wairau Road,
Auckland 10, New Zealand

Penguin Books Ltd, Registered Offices:
Harmondsworth, Middlesex, England

First published in 2000 by Viking Penguin,
a member of Penguin Putnam Inc.

3   5   7   9   10   8   6   4   2

Copyright © Cintra Wilson, 2000
All rights reserved

Grateful acknowledgment is made for permission to reprint "To the
Horned God" from *Witches* by Erica Jong (Harry N. Abrams).
Copyright © Erica Mann Jong, 1981. All rights reserved. Used by
permission of the author.

LIBRARY OF CONGRESS CATALOGING-IN-PUBLICATION DATA

Wilson, Cintra.
A Massive Swelling : celebrity re-examined as a grotesque, crippling
disease and other cultural revelations / Cintra Wilson.
p.   cm.
ISBN 0-670-89162-2
1. Performing arts—Social aspects.   2. Fame.   I. Title.
PN1590.S6 W55 2000
306.4'84—dc21   99-056496

This book is printed on acid-free paper.
∞

Printed in the United States of America
Set in Caslon

Without limiting the rights under copyright reserved above, no part
of this publication may be reproduced, stored in or introduced into
a retrieval system, or transmitted, in any form or by any means (electronic, mechanical, photocopying, recording or otherwise), without
the prior written permission of both the copyright owner and the
above publisher of this book.

For Elizabeth and Paul Gilbert

in loving memory of Kevin

Success went fizzily to Bernard's head, and in the process completely reconciled him (as any good intoxicant should do) to a world which, up to then, he had found very unsatisfactory. In so far as it recognized him as important, the order of things was good. But, reconciled by his success, he yet refused to forego the privilege of criticizing this order. For the act of criticizing heightened his sense of importance, made him feel larger. Moreover, he did genuinely believe there were things to criticize. (At the same time, he genuinely liked being a success and having all the girls he wanted.)

—ALDOUS HUXLEY, *Brave New World*

Of course, what made the whole thing smell was that many of the rich and famous were dumb cunts and bastards. They had simply fallen into a big pay-off somewhere. Or they were enriched by the stupidity of the general public. They usually were talentless, eyeless, soulless, they were walking pieces of dung, but to the public they were god-like, beautiful, and revered. Bad taste creates many more millionaires than good taste. It finally boiled down to a matter of who got the most votes. In the land of the moles a mole was king. So, who deserved anything? Nobody deserved anything. . . .

—Charles Bukowski, *Hollywood*

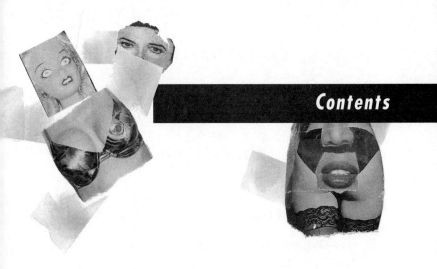

Contents

CONTENTS

Part Two: I Feel Pretty

Part Three: L.A. Is My Lady

Part Four: Orchestra Tickets to Grief

Statement of Intent,

or How to Read This Book Without Wanting to Hurt the Author

*A*round 1918 there was an influenza that killed nearly everyone. Before that there were locusts and frogs. There was an assortment of plagues. Once, a comet wiped out all the dinosaurs. There was a disease in Africa where people exploded.

Then there was this thing that happened to everyone in the twentieth century, where their insides grew small and weak and sad, and they all strove and suffered, and they sold each other down the river and fucked each other into pulp in order to obtain this thing they were all desperate for: Fame.

Some wanted it more than others; they were willing to push much harder, and were more ruthless and even more zealous than the others, and they were rewarded with everything the world had to offer: Constant slobbering attention. Obscene wealth. Armies of anonymous worshipers so hypnotized that they would saw off their own fingers just to be smiled at.

With the Fame came power and prestige. Those who had it were able to visually eradicate any evidence that they were ever slovenly, drug-addled, morally askew, or fat.

■

I wanted fame every day, for years and years and years. Every American has wanted it at some point in their lives. You can hear the longing for fame in your stomach when listening to your favorite music; you can feel your spirit reaching towards your own ultimate greatness, and the intrinsic undertow of millions of arms reaching out to embrace you, begging for you to come into their love. Weeping to clap and scream for you. You owe it to yourself, you think. You owe it to the world to be immortal. The sun feels right hitting your face in a certain heroic way. It is true that people in our world only grow to their seemingly correct tremendous size when constantly watered with compliments; souls become bright and shiny from an abundance of love and recognition. They unfold like golden flowers; they swell to pink enormity like jelly-fat queen bees.

Conversely, most nonfamous people are in a frequent state of dull torture from the lack of such boundless international adoration in their lives, as if they lived with a constant low-grade toothache, which makes us all grouchy and unkind.

Your auto mechanic who secretly hates you is only partially aware that the reason he hates you is because he is working on your car instead of being a famous and enviable sex symbol. Your barely concealed disgust with the rude, illiterate teen cashier with the fat, oily head at Blockbuster Video is only amplified triply by the nearby *Entertainment Weekly* cover featuring the expensively unkempt cuteness of Meg Ryan, who never has to deal with such people. Thwarted dreams of rock-'n'-roll superpower and oral sex in private jets are at least partially responsible for that nagging conviction that the world has been shortchanging every anonymous human since birth. As if to mirror the inequities of our economy, wherein 5 percent of the nation owns 95 percent of everything that is ownable, the overwhelming majority of our collective happiness has been stolen so that some goddamned TV teenager with oversized teeth can have more than she can ever use or deserve.

If a person in this day and age has two cents' worth of talent, it is considered his sacred obligation to Go for the Gold, to try and grab the big brass monkey ring, and otherwise make six to ten demoralizing career-and-connection-oriented phone calls a day, perform painful Top 40 Hits at all the high-school graduations and bar mitzvahs, pay hundreds of dollars for eight-by-ten photographs of themselves looking like sexually available newscasters, and audition with seething positive energy for every ExLax commercial that comes down the pike, until the day that the opportunity for Fame reveals itself like a pinpoint of light down the throat of a large python. When the fame begins to look graspable, when the hem of the glittering Elvis robe is visible through the thick red haze, the righteously downtrodden Fame seeker is suddenly licensed by history and common consent to achieve Fame by Any Means Necessary, and furiously lie, cheat, fuck, and steal his/her way into various cocktail parties and hermetic inner sanctums until the photographers come and the magazines call and the beauties in the restaurants swivel and wink and shimmer.

■

If you have any potential at all and you don't pursue Fame, you are considered, by yourself and others, to be unambitious, self-sabotaging, or otherwise too fucked-up to do what the good Lord built you to do; you are pissing away your natural gifts if you don't consider your POTENTIAL, which, translated into American, means vast, unrelenting MEDIA COVERAGE.

There is a little bit of talent in most famous people, even if they're only good-looking—something for all the attention to stick to. Talent is not, however, the reason for fame anymore, nor is it the thing one really becomes famous for—one earns fame by notoriety, or one gets fame by having fame. The good old way of getting famous was to be very good at something artistic, and have everybody fall in love with you for it. That doesn't really work now, because, as many critics have pointed out, nobody is very interested in art for its own sake anymore; now one only does "art" as a necessary part of the equation, the means to the end of getting famous, so one can get plastic surgery and go to parties in order to lick and be licked upon by other famous people like puppies in a basket. Nobody wants to be a real artist nowadays, i.e., a reclusive, self-contained workaholic, because it's no fun—you don't get enough attention.

I was raised in an era when people believed that they should get instant gratification for any small blot of effort spat out into the world. Young "artists" today seem to expect they should be able to drool out a batch of sophomoric short stories or a notebook full of crude cartoon heads and insert them into a Versateller machine and get a tidy wad of laurels; and the problem is, many of them do. This creates false expectations, detrimental to the process of Creation. Our greatest artists through history have always had to wade through years of being broke, misunderstood, and unpopular, spearheading the collective consciousness and having to wait in financial agony while the rest of the world caught up to their fast and advanced way of thinking. Nobody raised with MTV has any interest in this process at all. They want to skip all the difficult athletic parts and go straight to having their heads on the Wheaties box.

■

STATEMENT OF INTENT

Just because it is considered *retardataire* to trash celebrity culture does not mean it doesn't need to happen a whole lot. I realize that in the immediate climate, it is considered passé to bark out from a position of loathing for Hollywood and its monstrous by-products. The best and brightest pundits seem to imply that it is hipper to simply embrace Pop Life, even if one must bracket it in quotation marks and smirk at it through the lens of postmodern irony, and amusedly accept its rampant faults and perversities. Those concerned with "spiritual growth" seem to think critical flamethrowing is merely "negative." I have been accused of being addicted to the use of "attack words" to champion questionable ideas in this regard. I think that it is the perversion of this turn of the century that everything cutting or nastily true is repressed in the name of some form of quasi-Buddhist, ethical, and/or politically fearful good taste. In this New Age, Politically Correct *fin de siècle*, the implication seems to be that if you have any kind of audience at all, you're an unevolved creep if you don't use your God-given talents to promote Universal compliments and worldwide Love, and speak out in courage and compassion on behalf of endangered species and people who are stomped on and diseased and forgotten. (Yawn.)

I am as liberal as they come. I stand and vote for every gay, Green, peace-loving hippie minority cause there is. I think that everyone should practice being as kind as the Dalai Lama, and align their lives with a path of righteous example for the sake of all sentient beings. We should all hold hands and sing Bob Marley songs in Spanish and recycle for the sake of our seventh future generation and that of the animals, and these ideas should be promoted in all that we do. However, unless you're Jalal al-Din Rumi, these sentiments make for pretty fucking hopeless entertainment reading.

As far as this book goes towards being a method of helping the world instead of hindering it further, I can only state that here you will find, for the most part, feverishly lambasting criticism of our moronic culture today, which can act as a kind of stringently abrasive cleanser on your soul if you really have an open mind about it.

The slandering of iconage is a sport—not an act of aggression or bitterness, but an exercise. Why should these people *not* get taunted and roasted? We treat our celebrities, regardless of artistic merit, like an untouchable royal family, which causes most of us to act like dribbling serfs despite the value of our individual lives. We regard ourselves as slow-minded, vermin-infested bedwetters when presented with the gold-plated auras of media success in others. The implication of Fame, in this value-warped society, is: You've made it. You and your grand talents are so bright, you are somehow, both physically and spiritually, light-years beyond all us bone-sucking hacks. I yowl in disgust at this bias.

Fame is a perverse deformity, an ego swelling as ludicrous as an extra sex organ, and the people that have it, for a huge part, are willfully and deliberately fucked-up past the point of ever having anything sweet or human or normal about themselves ever again. It isn't necessarily personal; it is generally not the icons themselves that I jolly and assail, it's the huge tumescent aura of Otherness, the grandiose Largitude and supermagnified glamour of these deranged old musicians and dumb pretty kids and Sacred Cow Ornamental Personages that I attack. These people lead lives of fantastic abundance, a parade of constant fluffing and stroking and free stuff, and beautiful portraits and rare bouquets and plush red carpet and the adoration of brilliant, comely people they've never met at all the best parties. *This isn't anybody's Real Life.* Life is everybody's personal untrained hammerhead shark, full of thwacking emotional whiplash and spinal emergency, full of weighty grace and random threat.

I attack the maddening blizzard of tinsel scattered in the icons' wake; the tidal waves of false awe glaring off their shiny suits. I swipe at the lurid neon head of the amplified celebrity wizard and not the frail, dumpy little nebbish behind the big screen of fire, because we're all delicate and pitiable inside. I believe that deep down, everyone is fundamentally an OK Joe deserving of your civility and compassion, even the ones I really hate, like Richard Dreyfuss.

—*C. W., 2000*

PART ONE

THE HEART-TOUCHING MAGIC OF MUSIC

CHAPTER 1

Cock Rock for the
Twelve-and-Under:
Little Girls and the
Unhealthy Way They Love

Mother Nature determines what is poisonous to the soul and body, and sometimes it is easy to avoid that which is baneful and unclean: e.g., we naturally have no desire to eat fetid corpses or drink motor oil. What nature does not provide in the way of an instinctual deterrent, societal and karmic law handles by providing terrible disfiguring diseases and jail sentences and vast financial punishments. Without these, we would all naturally swerve towards being illiterate and obese sex-crazed criminals, engaging in heroin-addled blood orgies from the time we turn six years old, chain-smoking and eating nothing but bacon and cans of whipped cream and Starburst fruit chews. Our knee-jerk tastes, as a species, tend to swing towards the disease-causing, as opposed to the healthful.

In a similar way, the collective emotional palate of mankind at this phase of evolution is too skanky and immature to be able to readily recognize and avoid the fever-blistered hue of Unhealthy Love. When one is an infant, one can happily stick sand and garbage and house keys in one's mouth and feel an enormous sense of loss when they are taken away and replaced by a nourishing biscuit. The unfortunate human animal continues to hysterically refuse to advance past the crack-and-glue-huffing exhilarations of Obsessive Lustful Desire and to replace them with more benign forms of realistic love and/or intimacy. Nowhere is this more apparent than in the unhealthy love of rock stars by little girls.

Aside from soft-core romance novels and the emotional smut of movies like *Titanic* and *My Best Friend's Wedding*, nobody's ever been quite able to deliberately and successfully devise a hardcore pornography for women. *Playgirl* magazine attempted to invent it in the seventies, utilizing the primitive theory that women got as sweaty and overstimulated by brazen, naked pictures of the opposite sex as men did, and introduced a magazine with a hairy, brick-jawed brute in the centerfold, earnestly displaying his semi-engorged "Hollywood Loaf." Of course, the magazine was totally laughable and not particularly erotic to women, and *Playgirl* ended up being patronized more or less exclusively by gay men. The pop sensation machine has found the answer, however, to the age-old marketing conundrum of What Makes Girls Randy, and now all media outlets are saturated with bedroom-haired, cologne-marinated, undergraduate-age dancing boys.

Musician boys are invariably the first big crush of a preteen girl, her first big sloppy emotional response to the world. The creation of teen sensations is now a multi-national Moloch, and such phenomena as Menudo, New Kids on the Block, 'N Sync, the Spice Girls, and the Backstreet Boys represent a whole vital stage in the sexual/emotional development of the preteen—i.e., the kind of biological confusion and obsessive hysteria which causes little girls to wallpaper their rooms with gratuitous posters of dreamy, hard-nippled thugs and tarty kinderwhores and throw high-pitched grand mal tantrums until albums and T-shirts and concert tickets are bought.

Twenty thousand girls stood outside the MTV window at Times Square in New York City and screamed for teen-masturbation-focus the Backstreet Boys in the summer of '99, and a few days earlier, another twenty thousand girls stood outside the MTV window and wailed and wept and beat their breasts for multinational super-pasteurized Hispano-sensation Ricky Martin. America seemed slightly shocked, as if we expected all that weird screaming hysteria to have died along with the Beatles.

Preteen girls want two things: a crazed amount of un-warranted, worshipful attention, and something ridiculously exciting and magical to happen to them suddenly, which would enable them to turn sneering and tall towards their ignorant parents and various preteen enemies and have them all shudder with the recognition that they were critically, mortally wrong in underestimating the preteen girl, and that they will now Pay. The idea of this kind of powerful social revenge is so tantalizing, it is basically in itself a version of prepubescent sex. This fantasy usually extends itself into a whole obsessive scenario involving one or more of the members of a boy band, in which the following takes place:

1. First, the teen pop phenomenon receives the incredibly special fan letter from the preteen girl and immediately recognizes the special trueness of her love and her unique qualities. The icon falls in love with the girl from her amazing letter and school photo.

2. The icon writes the girl back and makes arrangements to visit her on the sly, in his private plane. (It is amazing the way the plane shows up in almost every young girl's whack-off fantasy scenario. It's practically a Jungian archetypal phenomenon.)

3. The pop star then spirits the girl away from her horrible parents (who die, tragically and bizarrely, soon afterward, leaving the girl with no governing mechanism whatsoever) and establishes an indelible love contract with her, which involves performing songs about her, songs from poems that she's written, and even possibly discovering the girl's uncanny singing and tambourine talents. The girl and boy star then live happily ever after, deeply in love, modeling together on the cover of all magazines, and they can buy everything they want, forever, and nobody can tell them what to do.

A Massive Swelling

All little girls know they will be kind and magnanimous and well loved when they are famous; all little girls are kind princesses and just queens. As it is with most celebrities, after the advent of their fame has camouflaged what an utterly unwholesome canker on the gums of existence they are and finally proven them Right in Every Way, they will gradually allow themselves to unbuckle their latent kindnesses and show the inferior people how a Truly Special Person behaves. There is a hidden assumption in all people, but little girls especially, that once all of their dreams come true, they won't need to improve their personality or character in any way—they will have been perfect all along, and everyone around them too fucking dumb to have noticed it before.

■

When I was growing up and in the prepubescent emotional stage that is the primary feeding ground of rock-icon phenomena, we had the Monkees (despite the fact that the show had long been canceled and was already in syndicated reruns by the time I was hip to it). The Monkees were great; they were goofy and moronic and they wore ponchos, and they existed outside of worldly angst and the hazards of physical romance. A date with the Monkees would consist of jumping out of an oversized box of Froot Loops and playing freeze tag with wigs in a penny arcade. My six-year-old friends and I kissed pillows named Davy, Mickey, and Mickey (Mike was too mature, Peter too doglike and retarded).

We just LOVED the Monkees. We never imagined
them without pants, but if we did, they had the same hairless nether-mound GI Joe had in lieu of an actual unit. We
talked about marrying a Monkee vs. marrying Speed
Racer, or marrying half-Mickey-half-Davy—it was all the
same. This amorphous nonsexuality was factory-built into
the Monkees along with the string you pulled on their
chests to hear "Last Train to Clarksville," and is the crucial difference between prefab-musical-teen-crush-bands-
assembled-by-teams-of-marketing-experts then and now.
Now, instead of castrating the stars, like the TV spin surgeons did to the Monkees, band creators imbue these
quasimusical teens with frightening levels of artificially
generated erotic power.

Children moaning in trained vibrato and writhing in
sexual anguish have always been a big attention getter for
old talent-contest shows like *Star Search* and other questionable TV experiences. On *The Mickey Mouse Club*, back
in the fifties, fresh-faced little teen vixens like Darlene
and Annette once sang unabashedly doltish ballads about
puppy love written by fifty-year-old men. The Little
Rascals dressed as adult hipsters and sang each other
speakeasy songs of cheap drunken courtship, winking
and wiggling. Now children barely out of training pants
are wearing asymmetrical Victor Costa ball gowns and
belting out how Their Man Is Gone in the smoky tones of
world-weary, dope-sick B-girls who've been beaten like
donkeys for loving too intensely. Naturally, most of this
can be blamed on the parents; overzealous soccer and ice-
rink moms have nothing on the white-sweatered harri-

dans who seek entertainment-industry success through their unblemished tykes. No bog-banshee wailing for untimely death in an Irish family could send more freon up the spine than a Backstage Mother howling darkly at her toddler in showgirl makeup, "Pretty FEET! Make PRETTY FEET for the agents, Missy!"

The recent rash of female pop singers have already figured out that crawling around in their panties on MTV is the best thing they can do for record sales. As singers proceed to get younger and more naked, child versions of lingerie bands like Vanity 6 are sure to ensue: undulating eleven-year-old boys and girls wearing Cuban-heeled fetish nylons and tiny athletic-support cups will be filling an arena near you, running microphones suggestively over their undeveloped chests, grabbing their unfinished nether parts, flipping their hair, pouting, feigning sadomasochism with the mike stand. Oversexed R&B tykes like Immature and Tevin Campbell have already been down this catwalk—they were boys who were not old enough to drive, who frothed crowds of grown women into surging jungles of wrongful lust. Somehow, to the wanton fan of any age, a charismatic stage presence means that the performer is possessed of a mature, diabolically supercharged megasexuality, and the fan responds to the performer as such, even if he is barely over four feet tall.

■

New Kids on the Block had a frighteningly sexual, Jesuslike sway over the female species. At the peak of their success, I remember, I read an actual newspaper column about how a three-and-a-half-year-old girl who had been displaying nothing but autisticlike behavior for her entire life was watching a New Kids concert with her older siblings, then suddenly snapped into lucidity, grabbed her mother by the arm, and drawled out her first words, her maiden voyage into the English language, a fiery demand: "I want Joe!"—Joe, of course, being Joe McIntyre, the youngest and shortest of the New Kids. In the early nineties, he was probably singlehandedly responsible for more kundalini-firehammers of sexual explosion in the twelve-and-unders than Elvis and David Cassidy and Mickey Dolenz combined. All of the New Kids, at one time, had to suffer being regarded as Emissaries of the Divine or worse.

I was once given a box of actual fan letters, left behind by a vacating fan-mail-distributing service, that were written to New Kids on the Block. These things were gut-freezingly weird and evil: they weren't just stacks upon stacks of love pleas from little girls, but bold propositions from forty-year-old women who had been sucked into the most terrifying brand of slavering fanhood by their preteen daughters. You could just see these desolate single mothers with posters of Donnie Wahlberg's shiny naked chest on their walls over the breakfast table, arguing viciously with their fifth-grade daughters over which of the New Kids was "more fine." Receiving countless amounts of these letters is the type of thing that would screw up nearly any boy under the age of twenty that I've ever known, forever—and just to prove it, I've supplied some prime examples from the collection that provide a fairly good overview of the bulk of fan mail in general.

EXAMPLE #1: *The Pink-Faced-Teenybopper Letter*

This letter, written to Donnie Wahlberg of New Kids on the Block, typifies a "normal," "healthy" fan letter. There were at least two hundred more of these, with minor variations, in the box.

All spelling and grammar in this and the following examples were left exactly as I found them.

All small i's in this letter were dotted with a circle.

Donnie,
hello!
My name is _____ and i am 17 years old! With this letter i have written 1,450 times "I Love You"!! Because i really do baby!! Not because you are rich and famous, but because you are Donnie Wahlberg!! You could be pour and not famous and i would still *want* you!! I got over 600 posters of only you, and i love them all! I think you are so cool! I love the way you walk, talk, sing, dance, well i might as well say I Love everything about you!! The other guys are alright too, but you are *number one* in my heart and soul!! I got everything there is on you!!
[Etc.]
I just want to say that you are the best and don't forget it!!
Well bye!!
Love ya lots
Your #1 Fan

EXAMPLE #2: *The Bored-Slutty-Young-Mom Letter*

This next letter, also to Donnie Wahlberg, represents another cross section of fans whom I still consider "healthy," if somewhat squalid and pitiable:

Hey

This will be the first of many letters. I am 26. + I also have two sons, one 8½ and the other 4. My 8½ bought a NKOTB tape. I admit I have heard your music before, I liked it but honestly did not think much of it. I saw you on that Disney special. I must admit, I really thought you were really tough looking. I have seen your tattoo it's a killer. I have two one one my left breast a rose on a vine. A butterfly on my back. I like to dance and stay in shape. Really only flaw, I can tell is that I am short 5'2". But dynamite comes in small packages they say.

My music tastes tend to run wild. I like Patsy Cline, Tchaikovsky, but I also like Warrant, Great White, Bobby Brown + especially Def Leppard. I am not a blockhead. But I wouldn't mind having a blocks head. Get me. I know I am five years older. But you know the song older woman. Baby let just say, I'm clean + don't believe in screwing around, I'm to safe. One thing I hate is condoms. But I use them until I am definitely sure. I like the real thing. I wrote to you on kind of a dare, I just wanted to see if you would write back. I have a bet with a friend, its between me + her, + now you, I will have you, just one night if you can take it. I'm giving myself a year. If you do write the letter it will stay between you +

A MASSIVE SWELLING

I. It's stupid putting things in the paper. I am no teenager, but I know what goes where and believe me I can show you.

    X

EXAMPLE #3: *The Drowning Teen*

Stop reading, all ye faint of heart. Herein begins the real squirminess. If you are a would-be teen idol, I hope you regard this letter with the same trembling and apprehension that Ebenezer Scrooge does when shown the tombstone of Tiny Tim:

Jonathan,

    Hi. My name is _____. I know you don't know me, but I really want you to pay attention to this letter. I really really need for you to know how I feel. Right now, I'll bet I can say that I'm your number one fan, and mean it. I'll also bet that I can talk to any New Kids fan out there, and none of them love you half as much as I do. Well anyway, about three or four years ago, I was a very happy person. Until I saw your cute little face on the cover of a tape that one of my friends had. Well ever since then, my life has been turned upside down. I mean, all I do anymore is think of you. I'm always miserable. I'm never happy. My grades have slipped rapidly, and every night I lie in my bed and cry. I asked my mom why the Lord made people so miserable. She told me he didn't, but he would only give you what he thought would make you happy in the end. She told me that I'd never get to meet you, because you won't make me happy. But I know that's not true. I know you'd make me happy. Very happy. I mean, you wouldn't even have to try. It would make me happy to wait on you hand and foot. I don't care if I never get anything else in my life, but I really really need you. Just to be a friend to you would bring lots and lots of joy to me. I mean since I've known of you, I can't picture myself with anyone else. I have no social life anymore. I can't seem to get you out of my mind long enough to even consider liking anyone else. My mom takes me to a shrink, but he's no help. He can't help me get to meet you. I really wish I could express just how badly I feel. But I've never been good with words. Or even writing them for that matter. I just want to take you into my arms and hold you and protect you from life's heartache and pain. I know you're probably never unhappy. I guess that's just what I want you to do for me. Sometimes I sit and think "Why am I hear." I feel as if my only purpose in life is to sit around and be miserable. I told my mom that I really want you to know my pain. She said he wouldn't care. But I don't think that's true. I think you'd care. Wouldn't you? I wish I could spend just one day with you. I know that's a lot to ask, but I've waited so long. When is it my turn? When do I getta be happy? When do I get to meet you? Sometimes I think that if I don't get my turn soon, that I'm just gonna give up. I'm gonna kill myself. The only reason I haven't already done it is because of my love for you. People always tell me to hold on to my dreams, and that they'll come true. Well to tell you the truth, I'm sick of hearing that. Of course I'm gonna hold on to my dreams. And I have been for a long time. But nothing's happened so far. I feel as if there's nothing for me in this world. And you're the only person who can change that. I mean just to spend one day with you. My best friend told me that I'd be even worse off then I am now if I met you, but again I know that's not true. Well I guess I shouldn't listen to what people say. I don't know, I'm just really confused about this.

Well I gotta go. I'll write again.

With Love,

X

(The signature is accompanied by a disturbing salivating cartoon head, with a talky-balloon that says "I Love You.")

EXAMPLE #4: *This Woman Is Out of Her Fucking Mind*

This is a genuinely unhealthy letter. On a fan scale of 1 to 10, 1 being the first letter example and 10 being John Hinckley, this letter is about a 7.5. I should explain that at the time these letters were written, the Gulf War was going on and the New Kids performed at the American Music Awards. Donnie Wahlberg shocked and outraged most of the flag-waving dolts in Middle America by brazenly wearing a WAR SUCKS T-shirt and sporadically grabbing his cock. People were really livid.

My Dear Dear Jordan,

I went over and visited with my friend today. She was very kind and understanding. I took over the book *Our*

Story [presumably the NKOTB authorized biography] for her to read. She is very strict and disciplined so I wasn't sure she'd want to see it. But she was just thrilled to see it. She wanted to know right away which one Jordan was. I told her the best looking one, of course. She narrowed it down right away to you + Joe, then decided Joe was younger than the 20 I told her you were. Now I see no contest between you and Joe. Joe is cute. You, on the other hand, are "Drop Dead Gorgeous!" I'm glad she isn't making any quick judgements.

Sometimes I think she has direct lines to God. She sometimes just knows things ahead of time. She wanted to know how my job hunting is coming along. This is just not like me to be picking up and moving across country. She said that normally she would have been devastated by my thinking about something like that. She said she is totally at peace with it. Of course, she has been right here with me watching my children be abused by their father. Her own husband, our doctor, had to report the sexual abuse of my 9 yr old. Then together we had to watch the law protect him (her father) and destroy the files. They have suffered through this as much as I have (Me—nothing—my little girls are the real victims here.) I can do nothing to protect them. Yes—moving across country seems right. Well, God has given me the will. He's put you in my path for desire and inspiration. Now He just has to provide a way.

I read in one of the teen magazines an article on the making of the "No More Games" video. It will be great to have another video. I can't wait.

A Massive Swelling

Oh, Jordan, I've lost 60 lbs now. I feel so good. We are going to the Y to work out at noon every other day. I need to lose another 40 lbs. My mom said that she doesn't want me to get anorexic. I wouldn't be the best I could be if I were anorexic. Besides, I finally feel that God is totally in charge of my life. I get scared and on real shaky ground at times, in fact, all too often, but things are just so different. No, things aren't different, *I* am different. *I* am different because you sneaked up when I wasn't looking and grabbed my heart. I was not ready for this. I'd have never been ready for you. I have to meet you.

Dreams have a way of shattering for me. There are times I just don't think that you are real. Well, dream or real, I love you. I wish I could know you better. I can't believe how you make me feel. You said at the end of the Fantasy special that you like to make people happy. Well happiness was not a part of my vocabulary or life until you entered my life. Now I'm smiling and laughing all the time. I see you on TV or the videos or my posters and my heart just flutters. I feel all warm and wonderful inside. I've never experienced this before. I really cannot believe what you do to me. (*for* me).

We are somewhat recovering from the Music Awards. My 7 yr old is smack dab in love with Donnie again. My 9-yr-old ignores it completely and surrounds herself with Joe + plunges into her books. She loves to read. My 12 yr old + 19 yr old are not so quick to recover. _____ is angry. She wants him out of the group and said she won't even buy any tapes of the groups he produces.

Her brother backs her up. I'm working on them though. She adores Danny and I told her she shouldn't take it out on any of the other groups any more than she should blame Danny. Then I also explained about Donnie having a real problem with the criticizm. If your friend has a problem you don't just give them the boot. They are trying to understand, but I guess he is really going to have to re earn their respect. You guys are in such a tough position. I look at my little gal's joy over Donnie and I can't help but like him despite his outspoken, harsh nature at times. My point is that we are recovering and still loving you. Donnie disappointed me, but you, Jordan, have never been a disappointment to me. I love you and "I'll Be Loving You, *(Forever)*"

Much Love,

X

S.W.A.K.

(Heart drawn around the name "Jordan," surrounded by smaller hearts.)

As you can see, the deep, widespread, and dangerous hysteria a seemingly inconsequential boy band can spread is absolutely staggering, and all the more depressing since the driving push behind the whole teen music deal is grotesque wealth.

It is a swell deal: all a savvy promoter with the naked greed of a pederast Svengali needs to do is find some mildly talented teens all lousy with fresh libido and stuck in some lame section of America, promise them a bucking, eight-second ride on the Magic Bull of Fame, and he or she can forge a sensational golden windfall as long as the kid stays on. After all that happens successfully, the stars might figure out that they are giving 90 percent of their salary away to some carpet-chested cigar aficionado who tells them what they can and can't wear all the time, and decide they'd like to try their hand at "going solo," a career move that has only really worked, so far, for the perpetually drunk Mr. Whitney, ex–New Edition R&B guy Bobby Brown, and now for Ricky Martin, ex-Menudo boy. The managers of the new breed of band coming out must have a whole clause in the contracts that says when the boys are too old and fat for the metallic plastic jumpsuits, and have squandered all 10 percent they owned of their careers, they are not allowed to appeal to any human tendencies in the manager and beg them for more cash to get back on their feet. There ought to be a Child-Corruption Czar in government, maybe. Somebody who can keep the pop machine honest, if not clean.

When Malcolm McLaren, the coolest of all the evil music producers, did his puppetmaster thing back in the punk era with toothsome filth like the Sex Pistols and Bow Wow Wow, he gave the world the impression that everything going on in his sphere was a collaborative group art project. He was a good chef about the whole thing; he knew how to throw together different talent elements while retaining the individual flavor and charm of the players. Even if he managed them poorly or tried to stick his hand up their blouse every now and then, he didn't quite eat their souls. (Well, Malcolm may have been partially responsible for the debacle that was Sid, but Sid was arguably old enough to know better.) The saddest part about the whole thing is how little true flavor any of these new young lover-boy bands have; they're wholly inoffensive. They don't stand for anything, they don't question The System, they don't introduce anything challenging or new, even in the world of fashion; they're as instantly pleasing and comestible and forgettable as a bag of Funyuns, and they all taste the same.

■

All of the frightful Pop Warner intramural seduction squads that are passing for music groups nowadays are really just dim approximations of an important event that happened long ago that kids today don't really know about. I don't really know much about it either. It is a historical event, and it is commonly referred to as "Mick Jagger." I didn't realize until viewing the video *Cocksucker Blues* by photographer Robert Frank what a king hell phenomenon young Mick was. By the time I was in seventh grade and alive enough to notice Mr. Jagger, he looked like a squeak-toy version of Don Knotts, and his laughably antique rock tours were sponsored by Pepsi and peopled by fat computer guys with baseball hats and Calvin Klein eyewear. In my junior high, only the back-parking-lot "loadies" with the feathered hair and bootleg cords had any appreciation for the Stones at all, and then even they mostly cared about the older albums.

A Massive Swelling

The loadies were baked all the time, so nobody trusted their taste; they also liked Ronnie James Dio and Styx and Quiet Riot and all of the other questionable schlock metal nobody listened to except other very very stoned people.

That video made me realize that cock rock was once very alive and is now very dead, and rock 'n' roll has lost its supply of frightfully charismatic young front men. Mick, Bowie, Iggy, Lou Reed, Bob Dylan—hell, Steve Tyler, if you even dare mention Aerosmith in that fearful lineup: they're all old, old, old, and it's a shame that most folks my age never had a chance to see those grand old gentlemen of rock when they were at their blow-dried, blow-snorted, blow-jobbed ultimate peak. The late sixties/early seventies is one era that will never really be able to repeat itself. It was an ignorant, selfish, sexist, self-destructive time. You could never repeat any of the back-stage action featured in *Cocksucker Blues*. Even the lowest slag-level of coke-and-cum-famished groupies have more self-respect than that now. That was an era with no boundaries whatsoever, and Mick navigated the ungainly sea of IV drug accidents and weepy orgies and omnipresent starstruck coke-gabbling morons better than any other lacquer-pantsed Glam King of yore. It is amazing that Mick was ever Mick, looking at him now, and it is doubly amazing that he wasn't found dead in a hotel room with needles in his feet and the remains of some horrible sex act stuck to his person years ago.

No white man could get away with that much genital focus these days. There was nothing reasonable about Mick at his gangly big-haired best, when he was wearing spangled body socks with extra codpiece sections for his legendary cod and long chiffon scarves and numerous cloth belts; when Lady Bianca was pouting around the dressing room, smoking petulantly in Halston dresses. He was completely without irony; there was something powerfully airtight, autonomous, and surreal about his ability to generate enormous sexual charisma which made men and women of the sixties and seventies want to immolate themselves against the fiery wall of his cocksmanship. He was, perhaps, the most sexually sought-after human on the planet at one point; a male Helen of Troy. The entire band was cadaverous from sweating off eight pounds a night and eating nothing but heroin; they were blown into wraiths from all that attention, all that masturbation aimed at them, the whole writhing mass of hippie culture imploding into death and debasement right in their hotel rooms. The Stones were a massive gale force that blew sideways the clothes and cash of anyone who came near, and Mick was the dervish at the epicenter, and it is hard to tell if he meant it that way or not, but he certainly survived it, even if his puckering chest and bloated features make him look like he's been shrunken by witch doctors in some form of unholy brine.

A lot of front men followed in the wake of Mick, but none quite matched his porn-star mystique. However, I was thrilled while reading through the box of NKOTB fan mail to find the following letter, written to lead singer Steve Tyler.

A Massive Swelling

EXAMPLE #5: *The Classic Groupie Nymphomaniac*

This letter, in my opinion, is perhaps the healthiest and best of them all, in that it leaps directly and gleefully to the only fore-seeable outcome/best-case scenario of the groupie/star relation-ship, i.e., a near-anonymous root job.

Dear Steven Tyler,

I am a big fan of you guys. I love your music. It sounds great. But personally I am madly in love with you. I know that you are married, but I just can't help myself. You are just so dam sexy and cute. I get turned on by just hearing your voice. I just love the way you sing. I am obsessed with your eyes and hair. Especially your lips. You just send chills up and down my spine. Everytime I see your videos on MTV I just go nuts. I just wish that you were not married. Because I would just kill to go out with you and have a love affair. You look like the type of guy who can make love really, really good. You look great in fishnet tights. I just love to see a man's body sculpture in tights. You have the cutest little ass that I've ever seen. Especially the cute dimples on the sides. That's another way I can tell that you make love really good. I could just picture it now. The two of us in my bedroom on my King size bed, and me lying flat on my back with my legs spread wide while you're pumping me to death. That would be so nice. Might I remind you that I have big tits and a nice ass too. I'm thinking about getting a tattoo put on my tit that says Steven Tyler. I'm sure that you wouldn't mind. I just wish that you could see me. I look much younger than my age. I'm 19 and people always think that I am about 14 or 15.

It doesn't matter to me how old you are. Age is nothing but a number. And you will always be hot and sexy. Older men are the best lovers to me anyways. They just know what to do. They make me feel good all over. It's just amazing how they please. I would just love to have you over one day. You would love my bedroom. It's like a jeanie's room. My bed has sexy see thru curtains around it and you have to find your way in. But it's easy. All you have to do is find the opening and just climb right in. Then we'll have fun all night long. I'll tease you for a while then I'll please you. I'm not gonna tell you who I am right now. I'll let that be a mystery. But think about what I said and I'll write back to you again and maybe reveal my name to you. I love you sweetheart.

Your secret admirer

■

I was at a rock show recently; a friend of ours got signed to a major label with his tight-black-shirt-and-hair-in-the-face alternative goth, wannabe-cock-rock boy band. Their black limousine was waiting with sinister promise out in front of the East Village venue, and hottie girls with long blond hair and silver boots were waiting for our friend to get offstage so they could casually smother him with girlish attentions. The lead singer was kind of a cross between David Byrne and Perry Farrell with just a skosh of Iggy, all of the boys were exceptionally cute, and the music was loud, but the night was distinctly boring. It was funny how unexciting it all was. One of the band boys got offstage and told me with guilt and horror that he thought he might have smoked too much pot. The twentysomething audience was barely drinking; they were worried about getting up in the morning and carefully monitoring their substance intake and responsibly choosing the right condoms.

There was a woman older than me in the club hanging out with her dad; you could tell by the relaxed and vacant look on his face that he had been used to way more intense party scenes than that polite little evening of hard rock, which was just pleasantly middle-aged enough for him to deal with after the abject chaos of 1971. Nothing actually happened in the nineties. Partying backstage with 'N Sync or the Backstreet Boys probably involved playing Tomb Raider II and drinking bottled water; it can't possibly have been like snorting a nine-inch rail of Methedrine and dripping candle wax all over the naked bodies of Van Halen in their heyday. All our unctuous songs of love on the radio are like the American dollar now, which is only paper, not having been backed up with gold for generations. There is no actual cock behind the rock anymore.

But there is one bold, fiery, tumescent approximation.

Chick porn, thy name is Ricky Martin. Love him or hate him, Ricky wears see-thru sweaters and has hips like a lazy susan. He runs his fingers seductively through his own hair, with his eyes rapturously closed and his moistened mouth barely parted, like Rita Hayworth. He is often seen wet, shirtless, openmouthed-kissing, and driving sports cars. Ricky is an emblem of virility and energy and soap-opera good-guy ethics, while being a near-perfect fusion of male cliché sexual images: one part Cary Grant self-amused privilege to one part James Bond eyebrow-raised-at-the-way-these-birds-just-seem-to-tumble-into-my-lap to two parts Julio Iglesias–cum Ricardo Montalban–cum–Medellín-drug-cartel Latino megasuave to three parts Elvis good-natured nuclear cock power, all shrinkwrapped into one silk-'n'-leather Milano-pimp outfit. He is a multicultural young Elvis for the new millennium, with hotter blood: Ricky, an ethnic minority, has actual traces of humanity. He's a little smarter than the old Elvis; he's already lived through the whiplash agony/ecstasy of flash-in-the-pan-ism as a boy who grew too many underarm hairs to remain in Menudo, so he has a sense of self-preservation and a healthy arrogance: he's not going to need shock levels of Demerol and pork to bolster his comfort level in the end. He appears to be a limitless, unstoppable font of self-enjoyment, professing an Internal Path and a Great Love of Music and all that other stuff. He has cracked the mystical code that makes the young girls cry.

Ricky has also claimed the abandoned scepter of John Travolta's Saturday-Night-Feverishness by pulling off a look that has up to now been regarded as either totally homosexual or ethnically slimy and stereotypically sexist: i.e., "Get a load of Sergio Valente at the bar over there, ohmigod, who does he think he is?" He has resuscitated obvious male sexiness from the way it disgraced itself in the seventies, when it wore open Qiana shirts and gold chains and pants so tight you could see all the veins in its schlong. Ricky has brought the sacred man-fire back to the pop stars in a way that those weepy, drum-beating-in-the-woods, encounter-group guys have been trying to bring it back to their own soft, gutless bellies for the last decade or so, and he deserves some kinda credit.

However . . .

I was all set to speak tirelessly of Ricky's golden legitimacy and flawless panty-heat, but I caught a little throwaway interview with him. Normally, when Ricky speaks, he's all chocolaty corporate cheerleading—for example, when he picked up his World Music Award in Monaco: "To all you leaders," he said, presumably meaning World Leaders, "you should take the music industry as an example—it's all about creating, not destroying." Idiotic, but heartfelt. Maybe forgivable. But later, he gave two spontaneous answers that made me think the Golden Ricky might be more hollow than solid.

A love-struck fan-girl interviewer asked him: "Who is your favorite singer and biggest influence?"

"Journey. Steve Perry," said Ricky without a beat of hesitation. Ooooch.

"Who is the most important person in the world to you, and why?" asked the interviewer.

Ricky then got an unfunny, paranoid shrapnel gleam in his big puddly eyes and started mumbling about how he always wanted to invite "his enemies" to dinner, because he wanted to keep them very close, even closer than his friends. The Wheel in the Sky Keeps on Turnin'. Wo-oh-oah.

■

I wonder if I'll ever see it in my lifetime: a whole generation of naked people too high to say no to anything, with some superlegitimate, undeniable Micklike Rock Lord at the center of it all, driving it all like a many-limbed Magic Bus. But when it does happen, I'll probably disapprove.

CHAPTER 2

Championship Karaoke:
Singing to Win

> From Pan
> laughing & fucking
> & making light
> of all devils . . .
>
> to the Devil himself
> the Man in Black
> conjured by
> the lusts of Christians . . .
>
> O for a goat to dance with! . . .
>
> O unicorn in captivity
> come lead us out
> of our willful darkness!
>
> —ERICA JONG,
> "To the Horned God"

*W*hile I like to embrace all cultures, no matter how remote, reveling in their difference and adopting their trinkets and religious idiosyncrasies and snacks of exotica, I fear that there is nothing to love about the god-damned dijeree-doo. Leave that noise to the aborigines. Dijeree-don't. If I never hear that wobbling burp sound again I'll be only too happy. Likewise, the Peruvian bamboo pan flute. Pan—the leaping satyr! Pan—Father of panic! Pan—with his pan flutes, gallivanting through the primeval forests of myth, arousing flame in loin! Oh, the laughter and randy skirt-hoisting! Maybe, once upon a time, it was OK, in a movie about the Amazon rain forest, to hear a mellifluous, airy tune being hooted through a quaint little panpipe while soaring over lengths of wild black river and tangled jungle majesty; but when you are in a subway, and some cocksucker in an alpaca pullover is spitting out "My Heart Will Go On" and emoting so hard the veins are sticking out in his neck, it's enough to make you want to destroy all young trees so that hamburgers and chemicals and cancer can prevail uncontested on the earth.

How, you may wonder, did I even recognize the Theme from *Titanic,* as popularized by songstress Celine Dion, when it was in such a heinously bastardized form, arranged for the Peruvian pan flute, as it were?

I will tell you.

Living in the world right now, unless you are building pipe bombs in a little shack in the woods full-time, you are going to be aware of a certain sedimentary layer of information. If you never watch television or listen to the radio; if you attempt with your every waking hour to avoid the Top 40 song list at all costs, you will still end up knowing every godawful lyric of a certain batch of bad pop music by heart, because you will be utterly unable to avoid it. Someday, you'll have to go shopping somewhere where some girl with hubcap-sized earrings who chews with her mouth open is listening to the radio. You will call your oral surgeon and be put on hold. You will live near a stop sign and snatches of heavy wailing will crawl from bass-heavy car speakers through your window with all the musk and ferocity of a heat-maddened rapist. In any case, you *will* end up hearing and inadvertently memorizing a lot of terrible songs, because several zillion people you don't know just love the living shit out of them. These invisible nations of people so love the Top 40 that they not only will wade through the barking retail-carpet and auto-body ads to listen to the endless rotation of them on the top Big Radio Stations that are piped like the Word of God into their workplace, but they will then, after their workday is over, go out and buy the same CDs for the full $14.99 price tag and play them voluntarily when they get home in the evening, in those relaxing moments that don't involve television.

The Top 40 has been dominated for years now by that royal family of singers who can twist all the air out of their larynx in an inhuman display of lacy, high-gospel vocal-emoto aeronautics and wild flights of forced musical hysteria, accompanied by string-heavy orchestrations and a commanding hairstyle blown into a backlit power-aureole by a large industrial fan. Often, leather pants are involved. Billowing white shirts are also important to their effect, which I suppose is to evoke the drama of being trapped in a strong prevailing wind, which I believe is supposed to evoke the drama of being tempest-toss'd in a fever pitch of heartwrenching that no mere mortal could stand. Their platform is an incredibly heroic dissatisfaction with Love, a ranting of Zeus-like proportions against Love itself, utilizing such universal laments as "I can't be strong," which is ultimately resolved through a revelation of forceful self-empowerment, such as "I will be strong," fueled by a lot of soft-jam vocal arpeggios. There is a tremendous need for this oversized, synthetic junior-high emotional wallowing. Teenagers all over the world rock back and forth on their beds, singing in hurtful little voices along with the radio as the cyberviolins choke tears out of their love-deprived eyes. Teenagers understand codependent musical statements such as "I will never breathe again" or . . . "walk again" or . . . "love this way again." This music distills the emotional torpor and the whining indignities of puberty and filters it through hundreds of thousands of dollars of production value into a kind of saplike audio cologne, which, for some inexplicable reason, appeals to billions of adults as well as the emotionally hairless teen. We are a Soft-Jam Nation. Walking into various shops, you start to realize that insipid, cloying lyrics with huge pop-symphonic orchestrations are the emotional wallpaper of the working class. "I'm down on my kneez, beggin' you pleaz, baby baby baby woah," etc., seems to pacify an otherwise disgruntled, non-movie-star workforce at their delicatessen and gas-station jobs and keep them in a semipermanent state of glazed, flavorless passivity. Listening to such music makes me feel as if I have just rubbed a floral-scented electric-blue toilet puck all over my face and neck, but I am a tiny minority in the vast world of music listeners.

Barbra Streisand is the monster that started it all. All those Top 40–sound Titans emerged fully formed from the terrifying loins of the Streisand. The world has yet to see another Tiberius-level, power-drunk control tyrant like Barbra, who executive-produced many films starring herself where the male protagonist had to look down at her as she was nestled coyly under the freshly dampened sheets and say, "God . . . you are so, so *beautiful*. Do you know that? Do you have any idea how incredibly beautiful you are? Look at yourself. [He offers a large hand mirror.] Have you ever seen anyone more beautiful than you are, right now?" At which point Babs, almost but not quite showing a breast under the sheet, mouths "I love you" through a thickness of beige lip gloss. The plots are always the same: Barbra, in some profound way, through her immense greatness of person, invariably saves Nick Nolte from himself or Jeff Bridges from himself or Kris Kristofferson from some unholy musical self-destruction. Aside from Barbra herself, who are these movies for, if not for young men to throw on wigs and reenact at midnight in some gay Christmas-ornament bar?

Streisand is an incredible sacred cow, capable of pulling indefatigable style boners year after year without losing a millisecond of love from the world armies of not-just-homosexual fans she has racked up over the years. Why? She's Barbra, and she is the prototype for that rare breed of totally irony-free diva, women who are so shimmeringly dead serious about the importance of their talents that they need to keep enlarging themselves with white weddings and entire clothing lines and personal scents named after themselves, every few years. The divas must expand like devil-yeasts or perish: they must dominate all spheres of attention and create others in their image and likeness to thrive and dominate after their own multiple diva-teats have withered. Divadom demands your cash, your love, your fealty, your not laughing at them. They are Classy, and possessed of diamond-spangled Talents, and you snickering little bastard-people are Not. Even Jewel, the little hippie girl who, at one time, it was easy to imagine running around a public park with bare feet and a dirty mouth, seems to be photographically going the direction of Celine/Barbra; falling out of an otherwise respectable pullover, hair daintily and angelically swirling in a religiously hued background, ablaze with ruthless cashmere superiority.

All the Top 40 divas-in-training share Barbra's tragic flaw. Sure, they can all belt the scuff marks off a stadium floor with their laser-punishing vocal instruments, but they all have the Kernel of Streisand inside that marks them like an uncorrected harelip: they all have incredibly bad taste. It must be the Faustian exchange they all make with Beelzebub to give them those spastically gymnastic voices. They all gleefully choose only the most palsied, pink-faced, shameful material for themselves, again and again.

Who can forget the softcore ego travesty of *A Star Is Born*, when the afroed Barbra turned her honey-pipes all husky and did an unspeakable chicken-dance for the hard-rock finale, a disgracing of the rock ethos unsurpassed in appalling hubris until the Pat Boone album *In a Metal Mood* well over a decade later?

Who can forgive the squalling nasal arpeggios of "Guilty," her duet with eunuch Barry Gibb? Or the whining dirgelike complaint of "You Don't Bring Me Flowers," her duet with the spinnaker-sleeved Neil Diamond? Or "Lost Inside of You," her puzzling duet with Kris Kristofferson (which brings to mind that old Tallulah Bankhead joke: Rogue gentleman in elevator mentions to Bankhead that he'd "like a little pussy." She replies, "Oh, darling, so would I—mine's as big as my handbag!" *Could this be what Barbra meant?*)? Or her tooth-peeling duet with eyeliner-pop-dreg Bryan Adams? Or her duet with (gasp) *Don Johnson?*

Yentl? Have the other Jews called off the *fatwa* yet?

Nevertheless: It is precisely the brazen obviousness and painful cloying of these aesthetic choices that bring Barbra and all Divas into the unshakable love of billions of music listeners; they are as tasteless and cloying as aerosol potpourri, and no greater a challenge to any décor, especially if you love beige.

It appears that the Streisand throne is being usurped by the morbidly shriveled and schoolmarmish likes of Celine Dion, who, despite her sexual handicap of being the most wholly repellent woman ever to sing songs of love, totally capsized the vocal world by trembling with pain over the eye-bleeding *Titanic* ballad, at one point the number-one favorite song of weepy teenagers and pan flautists all over the world. Celine is constantly surrounded by candlelight and weeping symphonics, and regularly engages in unctuous meowling with Blind Italian Opera Guys in loud emotional primary coloring guaranteed to choke up even the least sensitive or discriminating music listener. *(Christ, that was so bee-yoo-tee-ful! Get me a lotion-flavored Kleenex! My angina!)*

Celine Dion is one of the most freakishly mutated creatures the Streisand Machine has ever coughed out onto society. The stretched-out hair, the terrible bones under the angora, the black-buttered eyelids. The insane plucking and starving and discipline-greedy self-abnegation that she represents. I think most people would rather be processed through the digestive tract of an anaconda than be Celine Dion for a day, once they realized what a brutally unpleasant wasteland her interior universe needed to be in order to host such a deadly amount of the Fame virus. Quentin Crisp said of Joan Crawford that at a certain point in her later career, you could just see all of the raw terror and ambition starving through her big raccoon eyes. She looked like "a hungry insect magnified a million times—a praying mantis that had forgotten how to pray." Celine is even creepier than Crawford, somehow; Joan Crawford at least looked kind of terrified and in pain by the contortions of fame she imposed on herself. Celine Dion is apparently calcified into a form of orthodox masochism so devout that she obviously *had* to marry the frightening Svengali that was chain-whipping her into *über*-celebritude all these years, and she smiles the placid, tranquil smile of a woman whose every soft inch has some spiky metal clamp teething down on it; a woman like the protagonist of *The Story of O*, who at the end of the book is so totally, unbearably uncomfortable that she can finally sort of relax.

Since Celine is the new Streisand, she will at some point have to channel all of her massive selfness into film heroism; perhaps after her mini-retirement, after she's birthed something and found actual motherhood wanting in terms of attention paid to her. HBO will have her do some kind of incredibly moving portrait as the brave Mom of the fatally ill adorable child whom nobody understands. She'll have to clutch the blanket over the child's head while shouting to the schoolyard, "Can't you see he's hungry for knowledge?!" And everyone will think she's an incredible actress because she can make her big glassy squirrel eyes shed liquid on cue. It will be a big, big deal for everyone when she and the kindly doctor Make Love, and her exhaustively squeezed hair falls down and everyone gets a real good look at her naked, whippetlike spine. It will be a thrill that rivals when we finally saw Streisand's boobies in *Yentl*. Naturally, she'll have to sing a little. Maybe she can sing a Celine Dion song at a karaoke bar, which would be some kind of unforeseen postmodern coup of I'm not sure what proportions.

When she accepts the Emmy Award, her aged, unsmiling dungeonmaster of a husband will be remote-controlling her arm movements from the audience with a small steering wheel. When she gets back home to

Canada, he'll reward her by letting her jump for a nice three-pack of fresh nylons. Then she'll retreat to her little haystack in the parking lot for her five-hour rest. I can see her later, on Xmas, her favorite holiday, at the golf course she bought for her Master, secretly running away, away from the family and friends and snowmobiles, to go to a secluded section of her expansive estate among the trees, to shriek and growl and bare her razor-sharp teeth and ravenously eat bark and rub up against things. Once a year she is free as a chinchilla, away from all the horrible responsibilities of being ubiquitous, of being Mommy. Then her husband's henchmen will find her and drag her on luggage hooks behind the sled, back to the recording studio. And she will be glad—so, so, glad.

CHAPTER 3

Jacko, the No-Nosed Man from Motown (A Morality Fable)

Michael as well as myself have been severely underestimated and misunderstood as human beings. I can't wait for the day when the snakes that tried to take him out get to eat their own lunch and crawl back into the holes from which they came. We know who they are and their bluff is about to be called.
—LISA MARIE PRESLEY
(shortly before divorcing Jackson in 1995)

*T*here are people who, over their time of celebrity, have been seemingly autonomous broadcasters of a kind of Holy Joy.

Once upon a time, there was a little boy named Michael Jackson, who was a child of incredible, otherworldly talent. Hammered into superstar condition by a merciless warlock of a father who purportedly belt-whipped his musical ambitions into the hides of his countless offspring,

Michael was only six years old when his family's singing group, the Jackson Five, was signed to the Motown
label. He developed an ecstatic, feral-bird quality in his
prepubescent voice that transcended anything human;
he possessed the kind of arm-hair-raising sublimity
found only in little Anglican choirboys and castrati. His
big brown child-animal eyes and perfectly round Byzan-
tine afro-halo and his presexual, pre-self-conscious free
dancing suggested a huge pipeline into something other
and better and more refined than the filthiness of real
human life, with all its ill humor and defecation and
smarm. Michael became very famous by the time he
was only twelve, and got truckloads of mail from wildly
obsessed fan-boys and fan-girls all over the world who
wanted to touch him, kidnap him, steal handfuls of his
hair, and tear off his clothing and rub their bodies against
him.

In 1983, when Michael was in his early twenties, he
electrified the entertainment world by appearing on Motown's twenty-fifth-anniversary special with black flood
pants, cryptic diamond glove, and neon socks with
loafers, and effortlessly "Moonwalking" across the stage
like hot oil down a shingled roof. He was a revelation, like
Nadia Comaneci's perfect 10, that raised everyone's pop
consciousness. Fred Astaire called young Michael on the
phone the next day. Fred, all hopped up on tranks and
gin martinis, crumpled and gravity-bound like a pile of
wet newspaper in his hospital-style flex-o-bed in some
wealthy suburb like Burlingame, was watching the blizzard of inspiration that was Michael J. when he crowed to

his group of wealthy golf-bastard hangers-on, "Get me the Red Phone, the one that goes directly to the head of William Morris! I want to send that Nigro boy a shiny new dollar!"

In the next few years, Jackson became one of the rare and proud to achieve a substantial stretch of documented extraterrestrial excellence, like Baryshnikov in his prime, or Michael Jordan. Much of his older dance music holds up as well as anything in the timeless lexicon of royal R&B greats, particularly those songs from the *Off the Wall* album and the subsequent *Thriller* LP. Shortly after those records broke all previous records, mega-mega-megafame trained the deadly blue heat of its X-ray eye on young Jackson and stared him crispy.

With his new multimillions, Michael built himself a fantasy home: Neverland Ranch, named after the land of Peter Pan, the fairy boy who never grew up. Neverland Ranch contains a full-scale amusement park with carousels and Ferris wheels, two real choo-choo trains, and an entire petting zoo. Michael invited little children from all over the world to come and play with him. Michael lo-o-oved children, because his dad was a mean Jehovah's Witness and he never got to play or have Christmas or birthdays growing up; he only got ruthless beatings, and was forced to learn mature love ballads and complicated dance routines. Michael felt that the innocent hearts of children were keys to the magical secrets of life. "When I'm upset about a recording session," gushed Michael in an interview, "I'll dash off on my bike and ride to the schoolyard, just to be around them."

Michael loved women, too, but in a strange, slavering, idolatrous way that made it impossible for them to love him back: Liz Taylor, Diana Ross, and later Lisa Marie Presley and Debbie Rowe, the Mother of His Children, all seemed to care very deeply for Jackson while staying at least a six-hour plane trip away from him at all times. He looked wrong with anyone too near his body. When he and Madonna were each other's dates to an awards ceremony, they looked as uncomfortable sitting next to each other as two morbidly obese people on the bus. There are some auras whose size and radiance require miles of solitude, like a nuclear accident, and Michael's seemed to be one of them.

Michael began to get a whole shitload of plastic surgery, breaking his nose and reshaping it so many times it ceased to look like a nose at all. There were pictures of him in particle masks and talk of elaborate enemas. People started to wonder: Was the star a strange, fearful virgin, or merely swishy? Why did his voice never change? Why were his closest friends chimpanzees or growth-stunted child stars such as Emmanuel Lewis? Well, thought the adoring fans, he's a lovable eccentric.

Michael kept making music, but his own image on the album covers started to become unrealistic and preposterous. First the *BAD* album came out, then the *Dangerous* album. Apparently, Michael wanted to be regarded as Bad and Dangerous, but nobody told him that he'd never look intimidating with plucked eyebrows and rouge and the overaccessorized buckle-and-zipper ensembles which made him look like a rodeo dominatrix. His appearance was especially puzzling and ineffectual when compared with that of actual "bad" and dangerous musical celebrities like NWA or Public Enemy. Still, despite the slack in record sales and street credibility, things were going pretty well for young Michael.

Then, in 1993, a little kid started telling policemen intimate details about Jackson's weewee, and the tapestry of Michael's talented mind started to unravel before the entire world. Suddenly Jackson's eccentricities started to make *sense*. Ooooh! said the world. We get it now—the merry-go-round, the crying at *E.T.:* he's a pedophile! The tabloids went apeshit. It was too good to be true. The most famous man in the world! Even talentless-joke sister LaToya turned her back on Michael, telling the press that she could "no longer be silent" about her brother's crimes. Young boys came forward to defend their pal Michael, but when they spoke of having slept in the same bed with him in a friendly "slumber party" type of way, they ended up doing more harm than good.

Michael began wearing more and more eyeliner; his nose got even smaller. His skin, once a pleasant mocha hue, became the powdery color of meringue. He had a deep cleft hewn into his chin. He began collapsing a lot and being rushed off to various hospitals to be treated for exhaustion, dehydration, and painkiller addiction. Michael issued many, many requests for the press to leave him alone, especially the tabloids, who seemed to regard Michael as their personal whipping-pederast.

Suddenly there were numerous last-ditch, triple-image-spin-bypass operation attempts by his PR squad to rescue Jackson from being exclusively thought of as a nose-less hermit child molester, capable of inspiring even more fear in the young than his old pet corpse pal, the Elephant Man. He married second-generation Ultra-Fame scorch victim Lisa Marie Presley *(which was at least cosmologically interesting: Elvis was also one of the most Zeus-like twenty-two-year-old songsters that ever lived; he also, for a time, possessed the lightning bolt of superhuman Joy. The Fame smothered both men, overstimulating them into frightful husks of self-abuse: they both had to vandalize themselves, since the world could do naught but love them. Despite the difference in testosterone levels, Michael, for Lisa Marie, must have been reminiscent of Daddy)*, but the two of them weren't able to convince America that they were in True Love, and they divorced two years later. He publicly had two "babies," albeit suspiciously pale ones, with his second wife, a friendly nurse in his plastic surgeon's office, and insisted that they were achieved through some form of actual sexual intimacy, as opposed to being begot with a turkey baster for a brood-mare fee of $528,000, as some tabloids suggested.

On the cover photo of one of his CD singles, he wore a carpal-tunnel-syndrome wrist brace as a gesture of solidarity with "suffering children." Inside, Michael had drawn a sketch of himself at the age of six or seven, huddled in a corner with huge, overbright, trapped eyes, clutching a microphone for comfort, in the saccharine-precious art style one sees of crying children in patch-work overalls painted on plates in *TV Guide*, with the caption "Ask yourself: where has my childhood gone?"

This was clearly a bid for more compassionate under-standing by the press, but it read more like a crazily un-self-reflexive, backhanded plea for his alleged kiddie games of Doctor to continue with the blessing of the American public. It was sadly obvious that he had no idea how spooky and fucked-up the drawing looked; how ut-terly removed from the "normal" thinking processes of his fellow man Jackson was. It made the laughably severe image he fostered for his *BAD* album seem almost sane and workable by comparison. It was doubtful that even the uncorrupted children of Thailand (one of the last places his tours could guarantee ticket sales) could buy his all-too-sudden heterosexual-progenitor act. His mas-ter plans for renewed lovability were even kookier and less understandable than what he did to his own face. What was this poor, outrageously sheltered and wealthy man thinking, in his fortress of stuffed baby toys, mon-keys, and pain?

None of the images Michael had put forth in his previous albums were as weird or disturbing as the towering, Stalinesque statue of Jackson draped with bullet belts featured in the promotional video for his *HIStory* album. Epic Records pulled out all of the promotional stops and portrayed Jackson as some kind of divine totalitarian emperor-general, unveiling statues of him in several European cities based on the three-hundred-foot-tall Monument to Victory in Volgograd, Russia. The video featured people fainting and being dragged away, the power of the image overwhelming them. The public was confused: it seemed that after all he'd been through, Bad and Dangerous Michael still wanted to invoke our awe and fear, not our smelly, whimpering love. However, on his now-rare TV appearances, Michael, laying aside his new chrome armor, started pretending he was Jesus. He would sing with his arms out, crucifix-style, suspended above the stage in a white shirt and oversized angel wings. As he descended with his freshly ironed hair blowing back, children in white choir robes of all colors and nationalities would run to him. Actors of all ages and races would reverently touch his shoulder, and Michael, arms still spread, would regard them with tender messianic understanding. At the 1996 Brits, the British version of the Grammy Awards, Jarvis Cocker, lead singer of Pulp, protest-crashed the stage where Michael was being lowered singing and deus ex machina–like from the rafters. Two security guards tackled Cocker, wounding three pious singing children in the process. Cocker later issued a disgusted statement about how the music industry indulges Michael Jackson's delusion that he has the ability to heal because of his enormous wealth.

Jackson epitomizes the fullest scope of *über*-fame in the United States. He's lived through the whole gauntlet: the best parts of it in his earlier years, the worst, humiliating and scandalous parts in the more recent. Anything Michael does now just reads like Outsider Art—he has become as strange and isolated and deranged as anyone who ever walked or crawled through shock treatment. He's the strangest uninstitutionalized crazy person in the public eye since Howard Hughes. My fear is that now, instead of fading away like his natural skin tone, Michael will remain in the public eye, and his bids for world acceptance will just get weirder.

Back in the seventies, when a TV show started losing ratings, they would make some horrible medical thing happen to one of the cast members in order to curry audience sympathy: Laura Ingalls Wilder's sister went blind late in the Nielsen death rattle of *Little House on the Prairie*. Fonzie had some Evel Knievel–style death bid avec motorcycle, to-be-continued. The idea was to leave the audience hanging in a morbid, prurient limbo and grab that same rubbernecking interest that people have for major car accidents. This is now happening in real life, in a small way, with Michael's young seizure-prone son, but for Michael himself, I predict that his spin surgeons will insist he be stricken by a freak-accident-related coma, in order to cause a burst of previously latent, Princess Diana–esque support for the ailing star. Thousands of fans all over the world will then feel guilty for turning their backs on him and send him Mylar balloons and teddy bears, carnations and crayon drawings; and the entire Jackson clan—most visibly psychic media–whore LaToya, who would also be spotlight-resuscitated through the tragedy—will embark on a constant bedside vigil. LaToya will go on TV to earnestly beg the world to pray for her ailing brother. Michael will miraculously wake up after ten days or so, and he'll really want to talk to the TV cameras about his "glimpse of the other side." In a fury of Moonwalking-Towards-the-Light enthusiasm, he will be asked onto daytime talk shows, but his aggressively Old Testament, Book of Jeremiah–style rantings will not be copacetic with the popular desires of the New Age, and his messages will cease to be broadcast. Should all this pass, I fear that shortly afterwards, during a peaceful lull, Michael will suddenly, quietly die under really bizarre, mysterious circumstances; perhaps he'll drown in four inches of bathwater, fully made up and dressed in an Ice Capades unitard, or slumped over on his private Ferris wheel with a telltale can of Silly String and a Ziploc bag.

I was worried for a long time that Michael was going to die soon; nobody I knew thought that Michael could live very long, particularly in his disgraced Short Eyes state, like Wat, the no-nosed man in the King Arthur legend who lived in the woods and bit children. I had a pseudomystical experience where I had a strange vision of Michael's autopsy photo. In many circles, bootlegs of this would be a very hot item that would get passed around the sicko cognoscenti in L.A. the same way that color Xeroxes of the police shot of Kurt Cobain after his suicide secretly made the rounds. Jesus, I thought, it's the only way the world will ever know what the poor little guy really looked like under all those buckles, powder, and paste.

But who has raised more money for bizarre, esoteric children's diseases than Michael? Who can blame a person for having tragic (alleged) sexual leanings when they were getting morosely dank nookie offers from every gender of fan before they were old enough to read? Do people not see the connection between making young children—who have no idea what's going on with their own genitals—into objects of widespread, grimy adult desire, and the fact that Michael Jackson grew up to be a white faerie princess who only shines with tiny boys and monkeys? Such unwelcome attentions must have grossed-out young Michael profoundly, and rendered impossible any hope for his having "normal" relations, gay or straight, for at least this lifetime. And who has provided us with more evidence that Big Fame will fuck you, fuck you, fuck you in the head until there's nothing between your ears but a sour, translucent jelly?

Run away, Michael. Go to an island and live out your days in the sunshine. Disappear before we, the world's mean-spirited publications, kill you with our obsessive, smothering need to know you better.

CHAPTER 4

Las Vegas—
The Death Star
of Entertainment

The ancient delivery of transcripts from the Shaman says . . .
He who seeks the light becomes the guardian . . . and spreads
the hope.
> —SIEGFRIED AND ROY

Huh?
> —CINTRA WILSON

As a white girl, I feel a special fear when I see a certain breed of my white sisters. These are the girls with something a little too damp around the mouth, the eyes of a soul who is looking for the wrong kind of action, and babyfat that is no longer cute. There's an ignorant danger about these women-children, sucking cigarettes, smacking their jellied lips, fumbling keychains bearing miniature shoes and bottle openers and roach clips and acrylic trolls. They have mousy hair in the waning, damaged contortions of an old permanent and extremely pale skin, makeup in unnatural shades of pink and brown, huge breasts, and oversized T-shirts, generally bearing some cartoon, something in the I WET MYSELF ON THE BIG DICK WATERSLIDE or JUST GIVE ME ALL THE CHOCOLATE AND NOBODY GETS HURT! ilk. They have splayed feet in white Keds, shins widening like a rubbery V under their large, quivering thighs. From some matronly gene, they inherited large buttocks in the shape of a wide, flat square. This does not prevent them from wearing extremely short shorts and halter tops that betray thick handfuls of misplaced flesh, nor does it prevent their hunger for mounds of whipped oil, dripping meat, and buttery dough. There is willfulness in their sticky little eyes; they look like they want to consume anything they can eat, smoke, or get drunk on first, then have raunchy sex with evasive, mustachioed gun owners, then watch television. They speak the loud ranting patois of the confessional-talk-show addict, filled with aggressive slang, trumpeting out shameful viewpoints as a badge of raw individualism. Often there are unfortunate tattoos involved—greenish-black smears across the ankles and shoulder blades of A Flower or A Design, not reflective of any conscious personal choice. Often you see them with their mothers, who look exactly the same but older, with worse perm-scorch on their short hair and maybe more gold-dipped jewelry.

These women constitute a huge part of the millions who loved *Titanic*, and bought $150 orchestra tickets to *Lord of the Dance*, and like bacon in their tacos. In short, these women and their stubby, cruel-faced mates are the people who support all of the questionable taste in the world, and are why Las Vegas is able to keep growing incrementally larger and more architecturally pimp-attired every year.

The broad cross section of America that loves the Vegas stars does it with a childlike awe. I find it to be generally true that the people with the most hateful, inhumane, intolerant politics are suckers for the most obscene forms of guileless sentimental exploitation; there's something about the love of handguns and Jesus and Old Glory, astronauts and unborn children that makes a lot of fat, racist, ultraconservative hickweeds want to gamble and buy sweatshirts and get all choked up in front of some wacked-out, self-worshiping bloatus of an entertainer in a full-body tiara singing "Born Free." It is this that has made Las Vegas the most obscenely overblown Xanadu fantasy hewn out of pink strobe lights, beige concrete, ravenous fruit machines, and thong-clad waitresses on the planet, and home to the most interesting form of celebrity entropy anywhere: Vegas is where strangely ego-poisoned and laughable entertainers crawl off to live like Louis XIV until they're dead.

Vegas is the limelight graveyard for Caucasian fame-junkies, the only nether-sphere of big-dollar entertainment where aging closet queens and hypervain, sideburned Republican megalomaniacs who refuse to wither and crawl into obscurity draw their last, star-spangled burst of audience attention and surrender to their own brands of frightening and delusional multimillion-dollar gluttony.

It always blows my mind to discover that some celebrity has built itself a whole jillion-dollar amusement planet of a preposterous Utopian homestead where it needs to spend all its time in order to rehydrate its blasted-out stage personality. For a Vegas star, this is the norm. Generally the house itself is a glaringly obvious psychological portrait of the star's deadliest veins of hubris and Freudian handicap.

Wayne Newton, a.k.a. "Mr. Entertainment," makes a million dollars a month in Las Vegas. He brings it all home by private helicopter to his ranch, Casa de Shenandoah, where he keeps corrals full of Arabian stallions, kangaroos, a flock of albino peacocks, and penguins. The horses have their own pool. Wayne's million-a-month doesn't include sold-out dates in Reno or Tahoe or Branson, Missouri, where "Wayniacs" will present the head of their firstborn to hear him sing "Daddy Don't You Walk So Fast" or "How Great Thou Art" for the seven- or eight-hundredth time. Apparently, as a member of the American Legion, Wayne spends a lot of time trying to get fans to write to their senators and congressmen in order to get Senate Joint Resolution 40 passed, which would make flag burning a punishable offense. He also organizes a "National Day of Prayer" in Branson once a year, where there are rampant billboards of unctuous, heaving, spread-eagled shots of American flags urging America to RETURN TO GOD and photos of little blond children gazing heavenward, rapt in unlikely, prayerful contortions apparently orchestrated by their weepy, Jesus-stricken grandmothers to resemble those vomitous "Precious Moments" figurines. Wayne Newton is a flaggot, which keeps him firmly poised to retain the love of the jowly white masses and his status as Mr. Entertainment, the reigning King of Las Vegas, America.

Liberace, the world's fanciest fella, had a costume budget bigger than that of most NASA projects; his lust for capes dripping the pelts of rare Empress chinchilla and platinum Azurene mink spiraled in cost up into the millions, not to mention his need for lead-crystal rhinestone Batmobiles and two-thousand-year-old pianos that Franz Liszt slept in. Even his writing desk was an outrageous, cherubim-infected, French potbellied monsterpiece previously owned by fetishy golden gewgaw queen Czar Nicholas II, whom Liberace modeled his whole fashion sense after and grafted with the stylings of Glinda the Good.

Elvis, of course, was able to spin his problem wheels the hardest and fastest in Vegas, while wearing spangled Mayan sun calendars stretched over his Krispy Kreme–laden paunch, and sweaty muttonchops upholstering his swollen and porous head. He would sing "Glo-o-ory, Glory Hallelu-u-u-jah" with thunderously overwrought isometrics of Feeling, squeezing the air in front of him with clenched teeth, heroically wading step by heavy step through a pathos thick as spackling putty, and girls and women would keen hysterically, mascara rolling down their necks, clutching at their chests, trying to peel their skin off to be nearer to the King, until the superprofessionally tight Vegas game-show-horn-section music spirited him offstage and back to the Valley of the Dolls. There was no irony in the love that Elvis's latter-day Vegas audience had for him, even though he was clearly Another Elvis, not the guy who went to the army or married Priscilla or gleamed like sexual mercury on the black-and-white screen, but mainly an unhappy fat Southerner, spaced out on Demerol, working overmuch to musically emote like an ouzo-stricken Greek uncle at a wedding reception. His Vegas fans loved him As Is to the point of religious exhaustion, Vegas providing the older female fans with a comfortable outlet to be the same snot-streaming hysterics they were when they and Elvis were all young and almost pure, the primary function of Vegas entertainment being to infantilize wilted adults until they act like delusional, fantasy-stoned, preadolescent Mouseketeers and wholly suspend all of their irony, taste, belief, and moderate behavior.

I spoke to an older Vegas Hilton employee recently about the 2,900-square-foot suite of rooms that was home to the King while his Vegas career swung: "They had to tear out everything after he died," he said. "Elvis had completely trashed the place."

■

Two men who have seen a lot of Vegas, and who can own it any time they feel like it: Barry Manilow and David Copperfield. Nobody has noticed yet, but they are the same guy—the same nice-looking East Coast Jewish boy. Two mainstays of the Vegas entertainment diet:

Bad Magic and Bad Music. He's a mensch. Copperfield is Manilow with a bunch of whirling chrome knives, a Harley, a *West Side Story* fake Puerto Rican wig, and a big slathering of Clinique bronzer. Copperfield/Manilow is most likely a gay fella; the Manilow, his melodic side, gives nice concerts in New York expressly to benefit the Gay Men's Health Clinic, and Copperfield, the magic side, enacted a ridiculous beard deal with cyberkraut model Claudia Schiffer, who everyone knows was built by professional scientists and has no distracting human emotions. But the gayness of Barry Copperfield makes no difference in the hallucinatory twenty-four-hour dusk of the Vegas Universe, even to the homo-fearing crackers and their big white women. Stick him in a pirate blouse, and that boy, in either identity, can pack any auditorium in the world, at will, now and forever, amen, and it's just a matter of time before his hair gets bigger and his clothing starts to sparkle and he erects his own personal southwestern Taj Mahal.

Siegfried and Roy seem to best typify the kind of bizarre, hydrocephalic celebrity life that it is possible to have only in Las Vegas; they are completely freaked out on a vision of themselves as beautiful New Age twin-alien butterfly Emperors, and they are, through rude will, able to sell this myth to a huge cross section of humanity. They are both so ultra-coiffed and have apparently had so many surgical beauty enhancements that they look like wealthy, oversexed soap opera matriarchs, yet they assume the stance of being able to hold a mysterious, almost "masculine" power over their audiences. They are clad exclusively in triangular shoulderpad outfits from *Star Trek— The Next Generation*, midriff safari ensembles, or leather pants with giant codpieces and ruffly chemises. They are extensively photographed in Herb Ritts–esque black-and-white, pouting with big lamplit eyes and falling out of their clothes together. They live together in a vast desert seraglio filled with solid-gold international tchotchkes and lurid reproductions of the Sistine Chapel.

In one bedroom there is an enormous mural, executed in the Conan the Barbarian school of artistic representation, of a Merlin-esque God (replete with magickal dunce cap!) angrily spraying white jets of divine privilege from his fingertips, in order to imbue a hypermuscular, naked, semierect Siegfried with the power to effortlessly hold several chains with a roiling mass of white tigers straining at the end. Now, if you really wanted a heavy-metal-style portrait of yourself conquering huge animals with your God-hardened nether-chubby, and you had the means, it is the kind of thing that you ought to do for yourself, but perhaps you would only show it to your closest friends and lovers, lest they should get the wrong idea and think you a narcissistically crazed Barbra Streisand of a homosexual German beastmaster. In Las Vegas, again, this is the norm for preposterous, ego-drenched entertainers, and there are proud foldout pamphlets about it, and the crowd lines up in sold-out droves for the punishment, right after the jing-a-jing-jangling machines eat all their money.

■

Perhaps there is an airborne spore in Vegas which enslaved Liberace and now has Siegfried and Roy by the boleros; they all end up with the hair of rash French poets and the jackets of Prussian limo drivers, hewn out of sequins and semiprecious chandeliers. Vegas icons, sadly, once having achieved and become accustomed to the unlikely lifestyle of a combination sultan/rhinestone cowboy/televangelist, can never leave; children would laugh cruelly and throw gravel at them in L.A., New York, or Chicago. These huge stars have found their own friendly Gas Giant of a planet to lord over with their puzzling, decorative talents; but it is a Faustian contract—the natural daylight and lucid, mild realities that the rest of us live with will never reach them in the bowels of the Casino. They have chosen to wield their strange and dark powers over a small alternative galaxy with an unnatural fluorescent robot sun that is guaranteed to keep them lit all night long and never set until they die screaming, screaming for More.

One by-product of the degenerative Vegas Fame disease is a puzzling military theme that all of these great men of Las Vegas embrace at a certain point; Siegfried and Roy have all of their backup girls wear enormous Trojan windfoils on their heads, chrome breast guards, and titanium defendo-thongs. Liberace and Michael Jackson, independent of one another, both developed the same kind of fascist bellhop ensembles to express their distinct romantic forms of world control. The light-sick and camera-stunned Vegas heroes naturally drift towards nifty antique swords and nippled breastplates. This must be some manifestation of the terror that they feel before their lust-maddened audiences; they must need thick, ornate armors in order to feel brave enough to face their atavistic fan base. The Vegas star lives in a gilded terrarium, and is afraid of you. Since they are so Divinely Incredible, your fan love for them, ipso facto, must be capable of becoming so intensely deranged and overpowering that given half a chance you would charge at them with a sex-fevered Dionysian mob, claw off their $700,000 outfits, and start cannibalizing hunks of their living bodies with your bare teeth and hands. Run salivating in a blur of love at the stage and you may be impaled by a two-hundred-year-old Spanish rapier. Cry, worthless teens and fat women! Repent!

Once a massive performer like Elvis has begun to rot and ceased to be functional in his old rounds, Vegas is there, waiting in the wings with a forty-pound Blackglama mink-and-onyx cape, ready to throw it over the star's shoulders and walk him off the Deep End.

Michael Jackson is now hurtling towards the magical Death Star, and the punitive exile of the nether casino-worlds. It is clear that the deadly Vegas spore has eaten valuable parts of Jackson's mind already. It's all there on his Web sites, all the Vegas-wasting symptoms: the copper-plated Roman sentry uniforms, the unregenerate photo galleries of fan-blown Michael in billowing white blouse, mid-aggressive performance howl, pouting wantonly in eyeliner and Jheri Curls, in particle mask and huge sunglasses, avoiding the bacteria of his supposed "actual" offspring: "son" Prince, "daughter" Paris.

Michael Jackson has been sniffing around Vegas; he is already the singer of the theme song to the Siegfried and Roy show, titled "The Mind Over Magic." "Siegfried and Ro-o-o-o-o-oy! Oooh! oooh! yowp!" he sings with danger and conviction. "Siegfried and Ro-o-o-o-oy!"

Jackson is building his very own amusement park in Poland now, and is rumored to be buying a casino where he can have a new rhinestone animal kingdom and perform exclusively for sold-out crowds of the Forgiving; but unfortunately, it can't even be in Vegas. It is hard to believe that the indiscriminate Vegas, mecca for the most haplessly overcooked fancy-men in the entertainment industry, can't overlook Michael's fault of Man/Boy Love. Vegas will normally accept any recognizable face, no matter how artificial. It's not like Vegas cares so much about children on the whole. They are usually standing around exhausted at two A.M. with Pixie Sticks the size of mop handles while Mommy uses harsh language at the ATM. But, like panfaced, psychic succubus sister LaToya, the only place the Jackson wonder can get any play these days is in deep Eastern Europe, where they are too fatigued from the crippling air and water pollution to do anything but ignore even the most bestial peccadilloes and indiscretions. On a quest to determine what went sour for Michael in the land of Nudes on Ice, I interviewed a Vegas cabdriver, while being transported between the Mirage and the Luxor, and got what was probably the truest answer to date: "They don't want his black ass here," leered the sweat-stained, unshaven orc, baring teeth like ancient mosaic tiles.

It seems that, unlike Sammy Davis Jr., Jackson doesn't have the right kind of friends. Chimps, llamas, and Little Leaguers aren't the kind of miscreants welcome in casinos. They threaten the values nearest and dearest to Vegas's bigoted, swinish, and cholesterol-enlarged Christian heart, which are keeping The Man in power, the niggers down, and the cash pouring in from the Right Kinds of Folks. Deep in Nevada, just like everywhere else, the face of Big Brother is that of Ronald McDonald, saluting in front of a taut vinyl American flag.

CHAPTER 5

The Shipwrecks of Rock

A thousand thousand slimy things lived on, and so did I.
—SAMUEL TAYLOR COLERIDGE,
The Rime of the Ancient Mariner

Now, I know I'm no rock critic. I haven't listened to much "rock" or cared about it like *Creem* magazine's Word God Lester Bangs did, but I know a fame-induced ego disaster when I see one, swollen and ejecting yellow nerve gas out of its spines like a menaced anemone. I know that rock 'n' roll has done worse things to the creative men of our time than snowmobile-fuel huffing is doing to the ruddy Northern Inuit. Men of Music decline faster than others, and with many more crimes and sores and failings of personality. Three men stand out as being important to me, men who truly represent a Wagnerian heroic rocker ideal of building a great, divinely inspired personal edifice of triumph and then being brained and humiliated by big falling chunks of it when it crumbles and burns due to the foibles of human frailty. These men are GG Allin, Mark E. Smith, and Ike Turner. (Ego-maniacal, Paganini-inspired metal guitarist Yngwie Malmsteen deserves an honorable mention, but I could never find enough smarmy details about his tragic 1987 drunk-driving accident wherein he wrapped his Jaguar around a Florida tree. Besides, he seems to be sober now.)

If we are going to dole out top honors to rock-'n'-roll personalities-in-decay, we must first recognize and pay homage to GG Allin, of the famously disgusting and violent punk band GG Allin and the Murder Junkies, GG being the Father, Son, and Unholy Ghost of public-disgrace-as-art. In the documentary about his life, *Hated,* GG, a paunchy, substance-rattled miscreant, waddles around small performance spaces in an alcoholic black-out, naked, shitting on stage, punching his own face bloody and physically attacking the audience, who have paid to see his show, whilst riding the revolving door of criminal recidivism in and out of Rikers. The film culminates with footage of GG lying on the ground with a girl urinating into his mouth at a frat party, swallowing as quickly as he can, throwing up midstream, then continuing to swallow the rest of the skank's offering as enthusiastically as if he were lying under an open beer tap for free. GG was an outlaw of heroic proportions, too belligerent and revolting even for pity. Nobody, not even fat, ski-masked felon El Duce of the Mentors, inspired more widespread fear and disgust as a lead singer than GG, who died shortly after the documentary was made. The point of GG Allin, in my mind, was this: nobody can say GG wasn't proactively riding his flailing lack of control into some original dark, psychic arena. He can arise on Judgment Day from his pillow of vomit and shit and Jesus will know that he was, at least, an Original Man. After GG Allin, the half-assed self-mortifications of all other rock icons seem flaccid and tame.

■

Mark E. Smith, seminal icon and leader of postpunk band the Fall, is another important cultural disaster. The speed-smart eighties are really horribly dead forever, and nowhere is this more apparent than in the onstage behavior of Mark E. Smith, the former most bright and bilious lead singer ever. Mark E. is a legend, a real artist, who has put out around forty albums since 1978, most of them great, full of peeling firebrats of face-smacking poetry and Tourette's-ish eruptions of unintelligible rant. Mark E. had always waged a quixotic battle against True Fame and the big McSatan record labels—it could be presumed that his vigilant raging against all forms of commercial success and total disdain for self-preservation finally cracked him like an egg.

Smith, when I last saw him perform, was sucking wildly. His delivery manner, always a cross between the nastily erudite David Thewlis in *Naked* and some Dickensian speed-freak carnival barker, was distracted and fouled by the fact that Mark E. had digressed into a hapless, mumbling wino, holding a bite-damaged styrofoam cup with a sinister amber fluid sloshing onto his pants. He had a black eye and freshly missing teeth. He kept sucking on his bloody mouth holes and stumbling offstage, keeling onto the keyboard with his whole scabby forearm and causing the amps to whine. His face was backing into itself like an old vegetable. He had long dry dimples running from eye to chin—those vertically puckered cheeks that only professional junkies and unsalvageable party-slaves who have no vital nutrition left in their bodies get. The band was just staring at him, with that expressionless codependent-family look, the one that sits down and is deathly quiet when Dad is walleyed and vacant, threatening to pistol-whip Mother again. It was heartbreaking.

There was still something compelling about Mark E. Smith onstage, regardless of the fact that he was clearly no longer Mark E. but the Dark Thing That Now Inhabits Mark's Body. Mark E. Smith, despite his disgraceful state of being halfway cured into jerky, still sang exactly like himself, as if ghosting in from elsewhere in the universe and only using his body as an awkward and perverse telephone. This, I believe, proves that Mark E. was at least once a real artist; he created a uniqueness in himself that even he, despite his best efforts, couldn't kill.

About a week after the show I read that Mark E. had been arrested for beating up his girlfriend/keyboardist in a Manhattan hotel room. According to an online music news source, the black eye he had at the show was dealt him by same girlfriend—she had hit him in the face with a phone.

Mark E. posted bail after a night in the pokey and vanished. He skipped bail; his band evaporated with their equipment, and only the girlfriend showed up to return to the U.K. and commence the Fall's European tour. Mark E. was AWOL, with no money and no passport, a fugitive; the band was lost like a felt-tip phone number on a wet bar napkin.

I hope history is kind to Mark E. Smith, and he isn't remembered for leaving snail trails of tubercular mucus all over the stage and beating his women. I think the music industry beat *him;* it finally won; it finally forced the marrow out of his soul with a kind of omnipresent drip-torture. It is arguable that Mark E. Smith spiraled into oblivion to keep the Man from Sony's grubby mitts off his precious mind. Mark might just be a punk down hard to the end, who would rather heroically crawl looped into dribbling shame than ever live the sellout Bono life, singing stadiums for Pepsi in leather pants. He's either that or he's just an unsalvageable asshole, and ambivalent to the core.

Fare thee well, Mark E. Smith. Don't die one of those dumb deaths like Nico or Stiv Bators, and get hit making a careless left turn on an old bicycle. Leave prosperity your filthy, stained notebooks and cheat sheets, and no matter what kind of wet mass of free-form hostility on an ugly couch you may become, the words will keep you alive for the children.

■

There is more than one way to decompose before a live audience. When Ike Turner, famed wife-beater and musician, gave his first show in New York in twenty years, I went with my friend Crisco, a greaser of the highest caliber, a staunch social critic who wears his belt buckle sideways and swoops his hair all up like a buffet ice sculpture. Ike's return was an important moment that needed witnesses, Crisco argued. This was a circus of dismay, a terrible thawing of a career that should have remained cryogenically frozen in regards to the public. Ike was returning to the razor eye of the audience, sopping with personal disaster and swampy backroom scandal, like a known mobster making an appearance in supreme court, pressed into a respectable shirt and moderately priced shoes by his legal team. We all saw that movie, Ike, the assembling audience seemed to say. We know you trounced Tina so hard she had to become a chanting nam-yo-yo tape-loop Buddhist in order to relate to being human again. She does our Chrysler and pantyhose commercials because she's our HERO, and you're the leering stimulant ghoul that tried to rope the great woman down. Still, you're a rare creature; you are a persona who has calcified into one of celebrity's architectural gargoyles, and we appreciate the stone-cold creatureness of you, even if we are watching you through several plates of bulletproof irony. Go ahead, the New York audience seemed to say. Show us what's left of you.

Ike had a new wife, the first member of the band to Watusi onto the stage, who was a bleached blonde with a big flat wet mouth, wafting a willful marrow-deep perversion that was all we could talk about for the first ten minutes. She conjured images of a rusty trailer in a desolate yard filled with dirty toys, hedge stumps, angry dogs, and chicken wire. A womanchild born wanting to explore the wonders of Mickey's Big Mouth and the various places to stick eggs and cigarettes. Sudden flashes of super-8 stag films paraded in our minds, her creamy pink blondness decorated by fountains of rapture provided by eight hairy brutes and a wild boar. Her voice was a blister attempting the Janis Joplin third-degree burn. Her cubic-zirconium smile and desperate jerky dancing betrayed her desperate need for starlike attention. We wanted to wrap her in a white quilt and take her to live with the nuns, and blast some of the hardened dinge of Torrid Ambition off of her with a powerful fire hose. It was hard to watch.

Ike, in his infinite mercy, had made his bride an Ikette, and their bedroom conversations were practically audible from the stage:

"Ike, when are you going to put my name next to yours on the bill?"

"Baby, I let you sing the first three songs! What else could you want?"

"Yeah, but then you make me stand in *back* of the other Ikettes for the rest of the set!"

Harsh words about her clumpy dancing, all elbows and knees; her thin white voice; her genetic lack of groove.

Tears, vindictive bottle-throwing, drunken apologies, raunchy conciliatory intercourse. A few more quiet mean words while naked, brief argumentative relapse, reluctant truce, pills, sleep. This woman had clearly decided that such suffering was endurable, because Ike was her ticket to The Top. She was trying to stick her painted hooves in the same little stiletto dents that Tina stomped into Ike on the way up. As God is her witness, she will never take the bus again, and she has the big vulgar diamonds to prove it.

Ike stood in his famous "back to the audience" stance for most of the set, wearing a red Nehru-cut suit and an abundance of gold, flanked largely by the two other Ikettes, who were lovely African-American women, both seething with one part embarrassment, one part boredom, and three parts animosity. At one point, the skinny one was forced to give an unconvincing and overrehearsed soliloquy about a particularly feral bout of backseat "lovin'" that did not succeed in making the audience aware that we were all naked under our clothes. She had been dramatically instructed to scream at certain lines, and drag out the "oooooooo" in "smooth" and other such forcible entendre, but it was tantamount to a poor hypnotist trying to convince a crowd that a box of frozen chicken and a four-pack of Seagram's Gin N' Juice was the Feast of All Saints. No pants afire. Can't "Stroke It" with a plastic pitchfork.

The band drudged their way through some tepid covers—"Proud Mary," "Yakkety Yak," and other exhausted bar-mitzvah favorites, lending nothing new and nothing attention-worthy to any of the above, except for the one point at which Crisco leaned over to me and said, "Did you hear those lyrics?!" He was clearly shocked and appalled.

"No, what were they?"

"'Smoked a lot of coke in Memphis, Popped a lot of 'tang down in New Orleans.'"

"You're JOKING!" I screamed.

Crisco shook his head a regretful no. "'Popped a lot of 'TANG'?!?" What was Ike trying to tell us? That stock-piles of worthless virgins in the South whirred by him on a rubber conveyor belt, where he riveted out their hymens with his bedeviled prong in a graceless act of auto-mated lust so jaded and routine that the girls were reduced en masse to the moniker of 'tang?! I wanted to saw Ike into dice-sized cubes and put his nether parts into the institutional chili at a women's prison.

The last woman to mount the stage was a proud bull-moose of a churchwoman in a sequined Patti LaBelle prom dress, with a powerful and godly wail worthy of the old soul material, which Ike perverted to his own aim by forcing her to take part in a grimy sexual dialogue with him on the stage. There was something so *wrong* about it—you knew that the woman was the best singer in a sweet wooden church somewhere, the custodian of a voice that could pull down the mountains and the heavens, and there was Ike frotting over her with the balding tire-tread of his own vice-damaged musical smut, cor-rupting her divine talents by paying her to imply onstage that she was begging him to perform a lewd act on her that even *he* was shocked by, which by the end of the night, given the precedence of the backseat pornologue, the frequent appearance of his Club International wife, and his apparent history of 'tang poppin', could only be a moral atrocity too complicated and venal to imagine with-out an ambulance nearby. While she and Ike sweatily pawed at each other with viscous bedroom rhymes from across the stage, we felt as if we were watching the wings of an angel being dipped in McNugget sauce and chewed off by a team of alcoholics in raincoats, her halo tossed like an ultimate Frisbee into a churning lake of Shame.

Ike's tour didn't last too long. He seemed to roll up the rug and vanish again, shortly after that gig. I reamed him in a magazine review, saying unpleasant things about his new wife and his new show and his whole tawdry purpose. Having verbally sucker-punched a man infamous for unreasonable flights of rage and childish violence, I wondered what the eventual retribution would be, knowing that it could range anywhere from a libel suit to murder.

Instead, I got an inflamed e-mail from an I. Turner, accusing me of having 2 assholes and declaring:

"IT'S OBVIOUS THAT YOU DON'T LIKE A BLACK MAN WITH A WHITE WOMAN."

Who was this prodigy.net-using bastard, pulling the all-too-easy and totally inappropriate Race Card on me? My God, I thought, of course Ike uses Prodigy. The only people who use Prodigy are thirteen-year-old high-school students from the Bible Belt and Ike Turner, who must sit like a decomposing animal in the Teen Chat rooms:

"Hi, I'm Cindy Jacobs. I am a sophomore in high school, blond with a big ass and real big titties. Are there any girls out there who have ever kissed or touched another woman?"

Poor old vulture, tapping away in the dark with his wife whining at him from the big gold bedroom. "I-EYEke! Who are you talking to NOW?!" "Leave me alone, woman!" he growls, fancying himself as aiding the birth of Sensual Exploration in the minds of young ladies rupturing with puberty's clumsy bloom.

It saddened me that Ike thought I was reacting to his darkness of skin and not his bleakness of character. Then I actually started to feel bad, and sorry for him, and sorry for being so mean to his wife, who was probably a really nice person under all that bleach and animal-print spandex. Ike had surely done a lot of soul-searching since his bitch-slapping, coke-monster years. There was just no mistaking in my mind that he was somebody who used his musical powers for Evil, instead of Good, and nothing made this clearer in my mind than his own opening band, Little Isidore and the Inquisitors, and their sheer, guileless wonderfulness. They were local guys, bursting at the seams with Real Soul, in a hearty, underdog homespun way that nearly made you cry if you were tuning into the sincerity of it.

This was a group of diehard misfit characters assembled by the True Gods of Doo-Wop: various graying and paunchy guys with bandannas covering their baldness and pastel joke tuxedos, and Little Filamina, a sixty-plus-year-old woman in a sequined smock with big plastic secretary glasses and a tight ponytail in a terry-cloth knot over her head. When she opened her voice, it was as if a fifteen-year-old earth-angel with the highest, most sparklingly true baby-girl tone had come down from her golden desk at Mount Olympus Junior High just to share her true teen pain with us. We were wrecked. Crisco wept.

We stood and screamed for her after every number and would gladly have kissed her hem and rings.

Little Filamina was finally introduced in her true Holy form as Little Isidore's *mom*. One's heart filled with visions of a yellow linoleum kitchen in the Bronx charmed with the voices of a high-school boy and his adorable young mom and his friends who joked around with her, rejoicing in an atmosphere of sheer love of harmony and that silly kind of music that almost everyone has forgotten and nobody sings anymore. Music was in them, and it brought them real levity and joy, if not a whole lot of Cadillacs and blow jobs. True beauty sprang forth that evening like a perfect daffodil growing between the thighs of a slain hooker. We were redeemed.

PART TWO

I Feel Pretty

CHAPTER 6

Only the Cute Survive

*T*here is written evidence that in 800 B.C. there were ancient plastic surgeons in India, who performed skin grafts.

In the U.S. in 1827, Dr. John Peter Mettauer, the first notable American plastic surgeon, performed the first cleft-palate operation in the New World, with instruments he designed himself.

Plastic surgery had its greatest period of growth during World War I, when soldiers were getting their noses and lips blown off by new innovations in weaponry. Surgeons were confronted with the new aesthetic challenge of renovating destroyed faces, which they met with a plucky spirit of invention.

The idea that ugly or deformed people's lives could be transformed for the better by plastic surgery was essentially popularized by nineteenth-century plastic surgeon John

Orlando Roe, who remarked: "How much valuable talent [has] been . . . buried from human eyes, lost to the world and society by reason of embarrassment . . . caused by the conscious, or in some cases, unconscious, influence of some physical infirmity or deformity or unsightly blemish."

When silicone breast implants were developed in 1962 by Thomas Cronin, M.D., of Houston, the submissive sexual role of women was taken to new medical outposts: the willingness on the part of a woman to surgically augment her tits in order to enhance male sexual attention.

In 1969, a plastic surgeon named Hal B. Jennings was appointed Surgeon General of the United States under President Nixon, bestowing a sudden civic prestige to plastic surgeons everywhere.

Plastic surgery was once thought of as a drastic measure. In the nineteenth century, even the correction of a harelip was considered aesthetic (i.e., unnecessary); as time went by, the operation began to be regarded as reconstructive (i.e., necessary). In the late twentieth century, plastic surgery enjoyed a massive boom as vain personal insecurities flourished throughout the United States among the financially comfortable. Nowadays, America's version of "cute" has become so type-specific that Hollywood seems to be heading the way of Argentina, where all women are thought to be so unnaturally repulsive at birth that the government will actually pay for all plastic surgery—everything. Argentinean women all have big lips and teeth and tiny noses and no lines anywhere, except where their wigs tape on and their nails are glued.

A MASSIVE SWELLING

According to the American Society for Aesthetic Plastic Surgery, in 1996 there were more than 1.9 million aesthetic surgical procedures, or about one procedure for every 150 people. In 1998, there were nearly 2.8 million cosmetic surgical and nonsurgical procedures. This is apparently because the Baby Boomers began wilting, and all of them wanted collagen injections, liposuction, eyelid lifts, and breast and penis enhancements.

∎

The Japanese have consistently taken American products and improved them; but try as they might, they were never able to produce a slutty, wispy-voiced blonde with huge tits. From the likes of Tallulah Bankhead, Marilyn Monroe, Jean Harlow, and others, we now in the nineties have the quintessential evolution of Blonde, taken into nearly Japanese perfection by the wonders of science: Pamela Anderson Lee (before she had her implants removed) and porn stars like "Lexus" epitomize the Hollywood blonde as the ultimate commercial hard-on: the ice-cream-colored girl who wants it.

The American woman at her best in hi-tone commercial imagery is represented as either openly, joyously brazen and whorish, begging to take it in any orifice, or unconsciously wanton and bursting with fresh, childish, as-yet-undiscovered virginal whorishness, such as the fifteen-year-old girl in the Calvin Klein ads who looks like she just got punched in the face.

The ubiquity of these images is generally due to the

fact that Americans will buy anything sold to them by a heaving rack of cha-chas. Every magazine in America resorts to insidious softcore tittie porn to sell issues. At any given newsstand, you'll see European photography magazines containing artsy editorial pictures of topless eighteen-year-old models reclining on sports cars and hunks of unhewn marble, next to mainstream fashion magazines featuring pictures of eighteen-year-old models wearing nylon-mesh bra-and-panty sets, next to magazines like *Club International* and *Barely Legal*, which feature pictures of topless eighteen-year-old models reclining against something sturdy so they can expose the raw pink insides of their shaved cooties. *Cosmopolitan* has been sold by virtue of freakishly cantilevered mumps hovering impossibly behind swatches of designer spandex for thousands of years. All men's magazines invariably run a shot of the latest actress/vixen tumbling out of a man's dress shirt. *Allure* magazine commonly features midteen supermodels in bikinis pressing their breasts together in a joyful display of preadolescent lesbian flirtation. *Sports Illustrated* may as well change its name to *Swimsuit Masturbation Monthly* and be printed on oilcloth for easy sponge-cleaning.

While trying to find reading-type magazines in Hollywood, I chanced upon a whole new perversity in the realm of alternokink porn. Ever since a friend told me about the new porno trends in Tokyo of big expensive glossy shots of schoolgirls either vomiting or being penetrated in the nostril (?!), I like to check out the specialty smut anywhere they have it, for purely sad and ironic reasons. This magazine I found was hidden with the really weird offerings: oversized Latina bootie mags, gay magazines like *Bear*, targeted at those who worship pictures of fat, prostrate slobs with three and a half days of stubble growth on their chests hamfistedly jerking off on construction workers; *Pledges and Paddles*, an unusually rich magazine completely devoted to gay college hazing fantasies *(Then Biff and the rest of the Varsity football team laughed with deep satisfaction as they forced me onto my hands and knees, and made me pledge my undying devotion to the University. . . . I bit down on the rubber wedge and winced as I felt the branding iron sear my pert, vulnerable buttocks . . .),* and the usual vacuum-sealed three-packs of magazines devoted to eighth-month-pregnant women taking it from behind from big black guys in bus-driver uniforms. This new magazine, however, was the most shocking to me. The gimmick was not old men in clown masks eating feces, adult babies out for a ride in the big custom stroller, or a foldout guide to the filthy panties of the sophomore girls' volleyball team.

This magazine's brave shedding of porn normalcy and ghettoizing of itself was due to the fact that its models all had "natural" breasts, which they *grew* all by *themselves*. Disgusting. Artificial breasts are the industry standard: apparently there are fewer men who want to look at real breasts than there are men who want to look at specialty fetish shots of shaved, oiled, slutted-out feet.

∎

Women have always been susceptible enough to terror-ism by popular "beauty standards" that they will volun-tarily opt for foot binding, rib and molar removal, bulimia, and spending oodles of money on various cosmetic oint-ments. Now women and men of all ages are so comfort-ably alienated from their own bodies that a great many feel compelled to regard their God-given shapes as in desperate need of violently invasive surgical redirection. There is a widespread compulsion to reinvent the face or tits or dick or ass that they believe is the root of their in-security in order to achieve a New, Improved way of be-ing received in society—i.e., as a better-looking person. Judging from the leap in popularity for these procedures, most feel that their surgeries were successful, and most recipients are entirely happy with the work they had done and glad they did it, and everything is all better for them—they are brand-new people living in a better world that loves them more. After all, everybody wants to be loved, and we, as a society, don't love ugly people. In fact, we fear the living shit of them. Even mothers have profound trouble bonding with children who are cranio-facially challenged. A dearth of cuteness can endanger your health, even: I read in a magazine that in an obscure study of abused children it was found that they were gen-erally "less cute" than other children; their features were such that they looked more "adult."

I believe the skyrocketing popularity of basically un-necessary cosmetic alterations is a by-product of flippant *fin-de-siècle* attitudes towards the physical body: i.e., it became very hep to think of the body as a fun tattoo scrap-book and/or primitive dartboard for subcultural statement trinkets. As shoulder pads and bell bottoms were the shameful God-I-can't-believe-I-wore-that banes of their own decades, unproportional breast implants and collagen lips will probably be as difficult to live with in 2010 as those enormous "Modern Primitive" Micronesian tattoos from 1990 are starting to be now. The newfound popular-ity of plastic surgery among persons of nineteen to thirty-four has Radio Power Stations, between recycled Puff Daddy hits, advertising for loan-sharkish ways to "Get the Money You Need to Get the Cosmetic Surgery You Want! If You're 18 and Over." I fear that the same type of scam that had overextended young white-trash couples in its grip and forced them to stand tearfully around while goons took their plaid couches away for late payments in the eighties is going to hypnotize people in the millen-nium, except they'll be standing tearfully around when goons take their breasts away. But everyone will be happy with the fabulous way they look this weekend, and that's all that really matters.

There are many celebrity examples of cosmetic-surgical strip mining with a blatant disregard for any organic un-derlying facial or body structure, but rather than acting as a deterrent for cosmetic surgery, the frenziedly rebuilt celebrities seem to only act as further incentive for the surgery-inclined. The public seems largely unable to judge good celebrity decisions from alarmingly bad ones, and embraces most celebrity fads as reliable routes to the Good Life.

Courtney Love got wonderfully famous despite the fact that she was kind of fat and homely and chewed-up inside, through relentless tenacity. She started her career by terrorizing us with the fact that she, like so many other millions of American girls, wasn't *ever* gong to be a supermodel, or even pretty or even cute. She was able to sucker-punch the whole beauty myth, thrash horribly like a half-dead fish through her personal tragedy and rampant displays of public fucked-upness, and still end up on the cover of everything. The thing everyone talked about for a while after that was what a tragic political disaster she became: she killed her own mystique with sheer Hollywood cynicism; she didn't want to be a worldbeating feminist rock symbol, after all. Courtney unequivocally proved that all Courtney ever really wanted was to be conventionally *pretty*. She surgically transmogrified into antiwoman Claudia Schiffer and got a Republican bob and wore long lavender banquet gowns. Courtney revealed herself to be, instead of a loud angry girl with ideas, a vain sociopath who venally choked enough money out of the world to transform herself into a "pretty lady."

It all seemed to start when Courtney, a few years ago, was being seen with her best-friend-of-the-minute Amanda de Cadenet, and the two of them squealed around like spit-shined go-go tarts in the same dress and tiara for a couple of parties, getting paparazzied. Since de Cadenet is kind of a model type and Courtney, next to her, looked like the day-old rack at a Polish bakery, Courtney must have taken one look at the photos from this stunt, torn at her alternative, disturbed-person hairstyle, and howled, *"I'm* going to be the pretty one next time! As God is my witness, the world will turn on its fucking ear before I look that bad next to somebody again!"* It hurts all girls at one time or another, very much, to not be the pretty one in a society that prizes beautiful women above all things. I guess we hoped Courtney would be the one famous person big enough to stand up to that lookist bullshit.

Then again, it is true that only the best-looking "feminists" get taken very seriously. Gloria Steinem, in her youth, could have been Ilsa, She-Wolf of the SS. Naomi Wolf looks like a dish who should be on one of those little private escort flyers that litter the hotel parking lots in Vegas. Even Susan Faludi is sexy in a mousy intellectual kind of way. Nobody ever thought much of wallflower Andrea Dworkin's ideas. "She just needs some big black cock" seemed to be the prevailing opine. Courtney loudly loves her nose job, because it made her life easier: people "responded" in a better way when she entered a room, she argued. But the real question is one of values: why should anyone want or need the kind of power over an anonymous room that the complete removal of nasal individuality can afford?

I have read in popular supermarket literature, and sources even more disreputable, that the tip of Michael Jackson's nose is dead and probably needs to be amputated. The nose, macerated by numerous surgeries, is apparently black and blue all the time because the blood in it no longer circulates; presumably these colors are a terribly harsh and embarrassing contrast against his floury, opalescent complexion.

There is a ghastly, unsubstantiated rumor going around, which came from "a Hollywood makeup artist." This person allegedly worked on one of the last Jackson videos and swears that Michael has *already* had his nose amputated. I was told that Michael, during a recent video filming, was dancing in his whippy, robotic trademark style, and during a quick flick of the head, his nose actually *flew off*. It was recovered by a prop guy and returned to the gentle Jackson, who, mortified, clicked it back on his face and sprinted back to makeup to regrout the seam. The nose is allegedly an expensive latex craft with metallic bars on either side which plug into magnetic strips implanted in his empty nose hole. This is the reason for the paint mask all the time; Michael no longer has anything natural going on, nose-wise, at all. The nose serves as an air filter on all human beings, and since Michael dismissed his nose, he is in constant danger of microscopic particulates flying directly into his brain and causing instant death.

Cher has an obvious jihad against aging and the natural processes of the body, and has stretched her face so hard that she looks constantly surprised, like an ironed geisha. Her skin has been subcutaneously sucked out and starched and replaced with the same extruded polystyrene that composed the decorator space sofas in *A Clockwork Orange*. Obviously, nobody dares tell her not to. Nobody around her is brave enough to tell her to age correctly; nobody would dare suggest that she give it a rest.

She makes migraine-inspiring dance music she can't possibly enjoy, at her age—her whole crusade for permanent youth seems to be a masochistic contortion, fraught with compulsive terror. Cher, considerably over fifty at this point, is probably dying to sit on the couch in a terrycloth warm-up suit and eat all the cheese she wants and watch *Masterpiece Theatre* at night, not wear another Bob Mackie gownless evening strap out in public and be brazenly erotic again; but she *can't stop*. Fame-cum-sexual-attention is like a bad smack problem, at that point: you have to keep getting a maintenance level into the bloodstream just to feel a normal level of happiness.

The Lion Lady, Jocelyne Wildenstein, plastic-surgery monster, ex-wife of art magnate/co-owner of the Pace Wildenstein gallery Alex Wildenstein, is the current reigning champion of plastic-surgery clearcutting. Her photo shocked the world when it appeared on the cover of *New York* magazine; this woman, who everyone says (from the Before photos) looked like a wholesome Swiss cheerleader before the nonstop slicings, seemed to think of her face as her personal canvas for executing the most frighteningly morbid annihilation of self ever seen. Judging by appearances, she'd started by having her head transplanted, replacing it with a stuffed replica of Grace Jones, then decided that it wasn't "feral" enough. Then she thought she'd really go whole-hog, and tattooed new Divine-style eyebrows in the middle of her forehead and had her eyes stretched into Japanamation cobra slits, built cheekbones by implanting two elbow pads into her face, and bought herself three or four big wet mouths and had them sewn on end-to-end. Her hair, a big plasma-storm rendition of a bleach-damaged afro, seemed to be the last thing on her above the neck to have any natural components remaining. She apparently wanted to look like a Lion.

This picture hurt everyone deeply in the soul; it shocked us the same way that looking at the picture of the charred head of a wartime soldier in a Time/Life book did when we were kids, but way worse, because she'd paid tons of money and done it to herself. At least three nasty kitsch-addicted gay male couples I knew had the picture pinned up in their bathrooms, for the electric cringe factor: you just couldn't stop looking at it; you had to run away with the cover of the magazine and stare at it, alone. We'd never really seen anybody erase their true selves like that before, besides Michael Jackson, and at least he still looked sort of human, albeit female and white.

Celebrity photographer David LaChapelle, in a show at the Tony Shafrazi Gallery in SoHo, featured several shots of a popular transsexual model we'll call "Trauma," one of La Chapelle's favorite subjects. One particularly shocking photo was of Trauma doggie-style on a gurney inside a closet, receiving a hypodermic shot in the ass from a big black nurse. This was art strictly imitating life: there was a large and growing number of transsexuals and New York makeup artists who had been receiving illegal cosmetic silicone injections from an unlicensed "nurse" at her home in Harlem that summer. The "nurse" allegedly bought the compound off the shelf from Kragen Auto Parts and injected it directly into their lips, breasts, buttocks, etc., and had been providing instant gratification for those who wanted a rounder whatever for the pool party that weekend at a fraction of normal procedure costs. "She is an artist," the believers gushed; those in the know were flying in from San Francisco to have her shoot their parts full of polymers; the "nurse" was a legend, and her backyard surgeries were all the rage. Those who opted for the treatment didn't care if in ten years this risky body modification turned into lumpy rubble that could never be removed. Everybody wanted lips like Trauma's, which the Harlem nurse gunned full of silicone to an enormousness just shy of deformity, and looked like an inflatable sofa.

■

Women aren't the only ones who suffer the rubber-is-better-than-real sex-part discrimination; men with small schlongs are perhaps the most pathetically insecure people in the world, and are rampantly suckering en masse into the most unlikely penis-enlarging schemes, which are remarkably well advertised in most metropolises, generally featuring a sculpture of a naked discus thrower or other ideal physique, with copy encouraging men to get the "male enhancement" they desire. I tried to call one of the smarmy operations advertised to ask them how they did it, and they were just a voice mailbox with an outgoing message that was all furtive and sneaky, like they thought they were doing something wrong: "*Thank* you so much for calling. We *appreciate* the gesture, and *understand* how *difficult* it must have been to make this initial call. Your *privacy* is of the *utmost* importance to us, so please, tell us a *discreet time* to get back to you." They came off like a bunch of eleven-year-old boys diddling around behind the Shell station.

I obtained the following position statement of the American Society for Aesthetic Plastic Surgery:

PENILE AUGMENTATION BY FAT INJECTION:
Enlargement of the penis by fat injection is considered an experimental high-risk procedure, and there is currently insufficient data to establish its safety and effectiveness. . . .

The procedure involves removing fat through a syringe or liposuction tube from one area of the body (such as the flank, or "love handles") and injecting it into the shaft of the penis.

Aesthetic plastic surgeons warn that patients could experience complications, including infection, bleeding and contour irregularities. . . . Furthermore, there is no evidence that the enlargement will be permanent, since a large percentage of the fat transferred is likely to be absorbed after only a few months. . . . A.S.A.P.S. urges patients to view penile augmentation by fat injection as investigational. . . .

In other words, the surgery is not going to make anyone's unit longer, but it might make it all clotty and infected and monster-looking.

Another option is something along the lines of the Acu-Jack, featured in many men's mags, which I assume includes some kind of mystery ointment and an ersatz bicycle pump. My personal favorite kind of surgery is the one an action star known for model humping and sequel abuse is rumored to have, for those men who can't get it up all the way: there is a kind of bellows device in their balls which they have to squeeze repeatedly in order to get their pneumatic dong to inflate. It makes me smirk how thrice removed from actual sex pornography gets, at that point: using implanted rubber squeak toys to whack off with petroleum-based faux-effluvia onto glossy airbrushed and chemically treated studio shots of artificial women's secondary sex characteristics. Feeling guilt and awe. Soon the Internet and virtual reality will replace all need for actual human contact; a silicone-moistened cyberglove will replace the diseased and emotionally complicated human vagina, and everyone will be having safe solo cybersex with Pam Anderson Lee, twenty-four hours a day, in every country in the world.

■

Trauma's ugly apparently wasn't just skin deep, nor was Mrs. Wildenstein's, nor Michael Jackson's, nor Courtney's. None of them were actually "ugly" before the surgeries, but now, by negating all the natural architecture of their faces, they have somehow exposed their scarily infested inner selves in a way that their real faces would never have betrayed. We have never seen self-loathing or rude ambition so nakedly before; no pursuit of beauty has ever looked so viscerally wrong. No statement about the unforgiving, shallow gaze of a public that detests anything but conventional beauty has ever been so spooky. As a result of widespread plastic surgery we no longer have any concept of what age is or what it looks like; if celebrities are the watermark of how we see ourselves in terms of attractiveness and success, the message is that we're not allowed to relax and age anymore, but go down kicking and screaming and trying to remain as sexually loud and airbrushed in the collective consciousness as a Colosseum-sized centerfold until we suddenly evaporate from cancer overnight, dying prettily and suddenly, fuckable to the last drop.

We'll see what happens to plastic-surgery junkies in the next ten years. I have a hunch it will eventually be regarded as a bigger cry for help than slit wrists or a pill overdose. Nobody should EVER think that they look THAT bad.

CHAPTER 7

Women in Sports

I, personally, could not be more grateful or lump-in-the-throat misty for the WNBA and Women's World Cup Soccer and all the new, "legitimate" women's sports. When the flaming X-chromosome came down out of the rafters at the beginning of the first women's basketball game I saw on TV, I got all choked up. It's been a long, ugly time coming; it's wonderful that there are finally sports for women that encourage them to be sweaty and uncute and actually physically dominating in a public, competitive arena, as opposed to the alternative: more contests displaying feats of tit-and-ass roundness.

I think it all started with Madonna's Blonde Ambition tour; one couldn't help noticing that her biceps were perfectly defined and perched on her arm like ostrich eggs, and the rest of her was as ropy and braided as only the body of a hysterically obsessed fitness junkie who will jog in the rain with a fever can be. Soon afterwards, a new female appeared: preposterously huge, box-bronzed, superinflated Gladiatrix Valkyries with jaws like anvils and clitorises testosterone-enhanced to the size of walnuts and Adam's apples they'd have to learn how to shave around. Suddenly there were weekly magazines that screamed about the body culture these women lived for in big yellow lettering; the enormous burnt-sienna woman side by side with an enormous man, both in browning oils and nylon thongs, grimacing in sexual combat with enormous plates of steel, touting the bottled superfoods they consumed and starring in photomontages of the terrible, grueling lives of Spartan gym slavery they led. The Butthole Surfers, around the time that the truly frightening Ms. Olympia pageant came into vogue, used a photo of a female bodybuilder's crotch for their *Rembrandt Pussyhorse* album; it was as veined and hard and intimately uninviting as an old tree stump. Some time afterwards (in the usual amount of time it takes for the insights of the avant-garde to sift into the larger public consciousness), normal people started to entertain the suspicion that all of these champion women of strength and brawn were sick, drugged, and insane and quickly becoming men. "Ms. Olympia" became a region worshiped by scrawny, submissive male perverts and dominated by huge, bleach-blond ladies with Lucite-heeled prostitute shoes and faces like merchant marines'.

In response, the rest of women's bodybuilding rebounded back into their version of ideal "natural femininity," which meant the athletes began to take less steroids, and employ the use of grapefruit-sized artificial breasts that protruded from their overdeveloped pectorals like hotel doorknobs, in an effort to appear more "feminine."

Now there is ESPN 2, and the ideal shape of women has been preposterously retooled yet again. The word "fitness" now implies tiny, sun-blackened women with no fat or water in their bodies and breast implants bigger than their heads in fluorescent short-shorts shouting happily to the home viewers while doing vigorous one-armed push-ups in the sand. There are "Miss Fitness America" contests, which combine the worst and most dehumanizing aspects of beauty pageants with insidiously smutty, gymnastic antics disguised as special flexin' 'n' posin' 'n' lip-synchin'. These aerobic contests are generally dominated by any springy young blonde in red, white, and blue tap pants who can balance on her hands and throw her legs apart in a spread-eagle while flashing a wide-eyed, open-mouthed smile of naughty, peppy surprise to the audience. It is, sadly, like giving medals for the best table dance down at the type of squalid neighborhood nudie bar that has an unfortunate pink neon name with a stupidly placed apostrophe, like "Superstition's." These poor women, for the most part, generally come off as being so totally brain-damaged in the "interviews" that the whole event seems plotted by some kind of Talibanesque extremist group that wants evidence to support its conviction that women should be wrapped in thick blankets and kept in underground bunkers with tennis balls taped in their mouths, for their own good.

Whereas women's bodybuilding and fitness competitions are firmly established as the mirrorized peep show where bouncing, swaybacked, microthonged body-slags are viewed for snickering, fetishistic pleasures, the Olympics have always been the ivory convent where holy virgin sportswomen are revered with weepy solemnity like preadolescent goddesses in heathen countries. Oh, how the Americans love it when a little American girl takes home a golden Olympic medal. If she's young and cute and innocent, she'll end up everywhere: milk mustache, Wheaties box, Nike ads, dinner with the President, cover of everything. If she's not quite young or cute or innocent, or if she's a (gasp) dyke, she can own more gold medals than Rameses II and they won't do her a dog's ass worth of good, product-endorsement-wise; she'll need a computer day-job or an escort service to support her sports habit. But oh, a strong little girl can devour the American consciousness like a box of Raisinets.

John Tesh was in surreally offensive Teshian form that Olympic night: "Can you see them? Can you see them? Little girls, dancing, dancing for gold." This was the Reddi Whip poetic musing that Tesh dribbled over the blurry montage of airborne tiny buttocks and the barrette-covered kewpie heads of our "Magnificent Seven," America's colossally depressing 1996 women's gymnastic team: Dominique Dawes, formerly a cat-eyed ball of lightning, over the hill at nineteen; Shannon Miller, brimming with negative anticharisma, the face whose expression ranged from pain to scorn, fear to humiliation, boredom to hatred; Dominique Moceanu, the plague of cute, whom every advertiser in the world was circling like a vulture around a stumbling ibex, climaxing prematurely at the thought of pressing her into a plastic action pony with long combable hair; Kerri Strug, homely and afraid, who wasn't cute enough to be loved by America until she crushed her ankle with the bases loaded in the ninth; and all those other hysterically neurotic Midwestern girls who've never had a real life free of bulimia and blood blisters and chest binding and galloping tendinitis, whose growth has been willfully stunted like bonsai trees.

These poor young women must be set free. Who are the idiots who told them that winning a gold medal at the Olympics would be worth sacrificing their height, their self-image, their entire childhood, and their bodily comfort forever? Sure, they can jump and twist and handspring like superballs, but Christ, forty-five seconds off the mat they look as shrunken and needy-eyed as suicidal orphans in indentured servitude to the Peking opera. This malaise is only amplified by the chattering heads of their horrific stage parents with their inky tentacles of vicarious glory, weeping and sputtering and waving little flags with their eyes lolling back in their heads, awash in their strange addiction. This whole scene is in no way less shameful than the methodology of parents in Calcutta who poke an eye out of their toddler and hack it off at the knees in order to make it a more efficacious beggar. Gymnastics must be destroyed.

The gymnastics aesthetic looks like it was created by a bunch of dangerously repressed old Quakers: the unlistenable, frantically upbeat, German orchestral power music, the bad leotards, and the strange choreography, whose roots are nowhere to be found in the world of dance—all of this has developed into an absurd display of heroic suffering and contortionism and a mockery of teen femininity. It's something like a neo-Christian peep show, with hardcore ambition being the pornographic element. *60 Minutes* featured a segment on a sad, cushy blond former gymnast before the last games, discussing her relationship with her coach: "I grew breasts and he called me a fat cow," she lamented, her eyes still overbright with thinly contained self-loathing, smiling with only her teeth. "I've been bulimic ever since." Nothing exists after gymnastics. They turn five circles in the air and try to fly closer to the sun, only to be eventually defeated by gravity and puberty and spend the rest of their lives as travel agents with terrible secrets who don't work and play well with others. Case in point, the obvious misery of Queen Nadia Comaneci, the former world's most perfect, who was wrapped in too much makeup and emotional murk on the sidelines. This was not a woman brimming over with enthusiasm and love for the art form, reveling in the year's championship displays of craft and discipline. She still hated everything: her eyes stabbed out of their painted holes like sharp pieces of obsidian; her body language nailed her off like a condemned building.

There is some unwritten law in the universe that says that only virgins can be acceptable gymnastic hopefuls,

because once the women start to look more adult and sex-
ualized, the impish scampering and bent-wrist coquettish-
ness starts to look like the over-the-top beckonings of a
palsied crack hooker. Liquid eyeliner, buttock gyrations,
and the pain of sexual knowing looks anomalous and sinister on the faces of four-foot-ten faerie girls. At the '96
Olympics, the Russian gymnast-women, especially, had a
stone-ground, chain-smoking unwholesomeness in their
faces and eyes, like they were about to patrol the streets
for bored townies the second they got off the mat: "Hey,
American! You vatch Olympic on TV? You are twenty-
one, can buy Zima Clearmalt? Ve got pills. Get in van."
Rap music, tinted windows, lascivious scream-cackling,
legs at impossible angles hanging out the driver's-side
window.

The heart-wrenching biographical montages set to
overwrought piano music were another travesty: "Little
Natalia was ripped from her mother's womb with a set of
ice tongs by Communists and given to Dmitri, the man
who would be her trainer for life. Natalia developed her
upper-body strength dragging corpses up the harsh terrain
of the steppes to the local incinerator, near the ice cave she
called home. Dmitri would tell Natalia hourly during her
rigorous seventeen-hour trainings that if she stopped moving she'd be clubbed by wood trolls. Sleeping covered only
with used aluminum foil near a tray of radioactive beef as a
means of warmth, Natalia dreamed of the day she would
be able to fly. And fly she does. Winning is all she knows,
this tot-faced little angel, and if she doesn't bring home
gold for her country, her little body may be sold and con-

verted to shark chum." Cut to shots of Natalia rubbing rock salt into her bleeding hands, having her head shaved for lice, praying in front of a huge, green, dead Jesus.

■

America hosted the '96 Olympics like a bunch of neighborhood mobsters—we did everything but systematically crowbar the kneecaps of our opponents, what with the alleged bad lodging and time slots doled out to the Romanians, and the terrible din of bellowing hillbillies stomping and hog-howling with pride for their own during the routines of Other athletes. The bombing was perfect—an apt manifestation of all of America's ugly brutish power, our gracelessness, our dumb inability to be elegant in any way, and our caveman animosity.

We must stop taxidermizing children with steroids and propaganda and turning them into joyless go-bots. If we can't do that, they should at least be allowed to flip around to the music of their choice and put more personal artistry into their program instead of their talents' being tether-locked to the dumb specifications of a bunch of unlubricated clipboard Nazis. If we're going to ruin their lives, they should at least get to enjoy a little dance in the sunshine of creative expression before they have to begin the long years of psychotherapy it will require for them to become human again. Let those poor little women get drunk and lie on the couch before it's too late.

A MASSIVE SWELLING

∎

Ice skating is another excellent example of the dangerous abuses of the prepubescent female by the world of competitive sports.

I was at one of the women's figure-skating finals during the 1998 Winter Olympics in Nagano, Japan, where twenty-eight girls, most of whom were nervous and janky and fell down once or twice, slunk off to joylessly watch their bad numbers roll up on the screen like people waiting for biopsy results. Nothing is more depressing than seeing a girl in a tiny dress fall on her ass really hard to a gluey George Winston–ish New Age piano number, then get up and smile through the rest of her set, holding the crying fit in her throat like a dead rat until she can get away from the cameras. Everybody claps really hard at the end of such a program, because they know the girl wants to eat broken lightbulbs.

At the program, I was sitting next to some women in cloisonné-pin-covered sweatsuits from Los Altos, who were hip to all the nuances of the competition, most notably the malignant political rivalry between the international judges, a cold war whose tensions are made clear through warped and biased scoring. "Since Russia broke up into all those little parts and pieces, they all gang up on everybody else. They wouldn't even let there be a Canadian judge this year," clucked the woman next to me, scornfully. It was obvious that something untoward was going on with the judges, because of the bafflingly low scores given to certain girls, particularly those with any personal flair whatsoever. Skating appears to exclusively reward undeveloped personalities, and seems to work along the same ideology as the Grammy Awards: i.e., the biggest corporate Uncle Toms get the medals. Artists with advanced personal style need not apply.

Likewise, any kind of sexual consciousness, even when adorably tempered and retro-lite, louses up the whole program, according to the scoreboard. The judges will find any excuse to shut the girl down who looks comfortably female in the form. For example, in Nagano, some of the girls used great old music, burlesquey brass numbers from the 1930s with oboes and castanets. "Ooh, they'll take points off for that," said the woman next to me. "You can hear that record popping. Sounds like a dirty needle."

No such points ever get taken off for the overwrought, totally digitally remastered Spielbergian Happy Meal orchestrations that accompany good little prepubescent windup tykes like Tara Lipinski or Michelle Kwan, the gold and silver medalists at the Nagano Olympics. They were both experts in exactly what the judges love: beauty-pageant smiling and coloring-inside-the-lines, suck-ass showmanship. Both bored the fuck out of me, really. Tara, the gold medalist, was just a puppy, a little kid, a lucky, two-dimensional baby champion with a tiny body and a big head, who knew nothing but indoor ice rinks and flash cubes and worldly reward. Her moves were pure animal skill unclouded by serious artistry or personality, because she didn't really have a personality yet. You could see it in her face when she jumped; she was always surprising herself and screaming like a game-show contestant when she got the highest scores. She'd never tasted any doubt, never felt her body do anything she hadn't radio-controlled like a hobby car. Wait until Tara grows, I kept thinking. Wait until she goes through puberty. Look what puberty did to Nadia C., or Oksana Baiul.

France's Surya Bonaly, the beautiful black ice skater, has gotten screwed by the judges every time I've ever seen her compete. Surya Bonaly is a blazing star, she is Josephine Baker, and should be dragged around topless on her skates by a snow leopard to Perez Prado rumbas. Her energy is snazzy, suave, and whimsically erotic. She even makes falling on her ass look Parisienne. She always laughs a sophisticated laugh to herself while watching her low scores roll up; she's a truly Teflon glamour-puss, a great lover of the ironies of life and sport, and the judges can't stand her. In a similar way, watching Lu Chen is like seeing a beautiful Hong Kong movie star do outlandish stunts in a tight red dress, subtly emoting the whole time in an irresistible, Ginger Rogers kind of way—a small eye roll, a little chiffon hip flounce—and she always gets belt-whipped by the judges like a dyslexic stepchild, and mysteriously never places better than bronze.

A friend of mine, while watching an earlier Winter Olympic games and noting the ungodly aesthetic restrictions placed on figure skating by the ancient judging criteria, remarked that Tonya Harding, in order to properly serve her craft, really needed to skate around in a cutoff T-shirt and thong to music by Biohazard. This idea, like all other good ones, leaked out into the cosmos through the powers of osmosis, and for a while, professional figure skating had a blistering commercial renaissance as an oversexed wet explosion of Raw Rock-'n'-Roll Power. Tonya still isn't allowed to play with the other girls, but she was the slain messenger that first brought the filthy rock-'n'-roll vibe to the ice castle—along with an infusion of crime and pornography. Since then, that frozen avenue of sport has undergone a startling neon transformation, and has moved from being a clinical display of God-fearing athletic discipline to a raging Vegas stunt orgy not unlike the futuristic world of the techno-roller musical *Starlight Express*.

It's only natural that Kristy Yamaguchi and Nancy Kerrigan and Oksana Baiul and all those foreign guys named Elvis and the countless blow-dried ballroom-skate couples would abandon all the divine respect the amateur world of sports has to offer and go straight for the huge money, the vinyl tube tops and the Springsteen music and the Freedom to punch the air in a pair of fingerless leather gloves. Unfortunately, this new artistic liberation has been translated by the former Olympic princesses in their new choreographies into a lot of awkward spine-jerking and pelvic unctuation and graceless burlesque moves from the Gypsy Rose Lee era of repressed tease-stripping. The girls, despite the oily budding of their new MTV sensuality, still seem to be held in ironclad check by the gravitational weight of Paternal Shame cast down by the glass-eating old Presbyterians that still judge these events. There is a staunch refusal from the Authorities controlling events like the World Professional Skating Championship and the various ice-dancing competitions to relinquish hold of the nostalgia for the clean, cubist ice sportiness that horsey Mormon types like Dorothy Hamill and JoJo Starbuck originated back in the seventies. There is still that big unwritten virgin/slut law, which is obvious if you've ever caught a few minutes of the competitions: a woman who comes off as sexually cognizant can do a brilliant, moody ice routine to a slow Portishead number, while wearing candy-apple-red hot pants and a macramé halter, and she may be amazing, she may be the chilled version of Martha Graham, and she may dominate the contest—*for a second*...but *then* the frigid Asian teen beauty in the midi-length pink chiffon skirt will slide out of the hatch and start twirling inanely to the love theme from *The Lion King* with pink disco lights swarming about her like animated cherry blossoms, at which point the entire sports universe says "Aaaw!" and grants her two million dollars in product endorsements, and she comes in first, out of fealty to the smarmy-sweet Christian tenderness that is the silent tyranny over all ice-dancing events. The "experienced" women of ice are punished for their sophistication; they are still being pelted with moralistic gravel and given no gold, only bronze, which they are forced to wear around their necks like a scarlet A.

This is the kind of dangerous hypocrisy and whiplash virgin/whore shape shifting that generate tragedies like JonBenet Ramsey and magazines like *Barely Legal:* the public craves the Sweet Sixteen Disney Bridesmaid, the smell of a new Ballerina Barbie, the white dress with the thin pink ribbons and the tumbling locks of floral-scented blond. Then we require her to go through the Olivia Newton-John metamorphosis at the end of *Grease* and emerge as a ruthless, self-empowered dominatrix in a black latex body condom: we want a willful initiation of the defiling process, by the virgin herself. From that moment on, she'll always get second or third place in the tournament, but she'll never have more power in her whole life than at that one moment, when she turns pro and lifts the veil of virgin mystery and shows the world her cookies for the first time. We want all our gold medalists to step out onto the frozen landscape like preadolescent baboons in estrus now that they've gone pro, everything bursting with fresh, unsullied sex drive packed in spandex. Go for it, girls! The word "pro," when applied to a skater, somehow assumes the same dirty connotation that it would when applied to a too-good-looking chick in a skimpy dress alone at a hotel bar.

Give me Oksana Baiul and her sloppy drunken blubbering any day over mechanized, kiss-ass, teen super-clerks like Tara Lipinski. At least she had a soul, even if it was a little dirty. "Professional Status" was indirectly blamed for histrionic ice teen Oksana's drunken totaling of her Mercedes. Her friends defended Oksana, implying that although her blood-alcohol level was soaring above the legal limit, her crash should be attributed to the bipolar emotionality of her weepy love for the music of Madonna. I remember Oksana at her Olympics. She'd turn purple and start screaming as if her legs were being twisted off, arching her back and not breathing and tear-ing the hair out of the arms of her coach/surrogate mother every time she got off the ice, and that was to music she probably didn't like at all. "She got too much too fast," clucked her handlers, referring to her $million-plus professional contract, and the fact that she had apparently forsaken practicing skating fourteen hours a day like the forlorn orphan she was for nightclubbing and boyfriends and unchecked alcohol consumption. It was a given that someone with Oksana's miserable history would want to come to America and become Shannen Doherty. She skated her whole life to be a beautiful rich drunk girl with a Mercedes, and only our obscenely moneyed pro circuit could let her realize her dream. She's one of Us now.

There are skaters who have been perfectly attuned to the sudden aesthetic transformation from holy amateur to professional skank: Scott Hamilton has always looked to me like some kind of thinly concealed Jiminy Cricket pervert, with his tight spangled pants and Claymation-elf A-OK rinkside manner; but it is the opinion of this author that Oksana Baiul is a histrionic poet drunk and a serious artist, and she really needed to be yanked from the circuit altogether and given antidepressants and taught gardening and put on a strict regimen of Emerson and Coleridge in a place like Findhorn Garden, where she could meet older men who would talk to her patiently about physics so she wouldn't end up in dark little boxes in the middle of the night with vampires like Matt Dillon.

Tonya Harding is the martyr of all skating women, with her grubby impulses and Jerry Springer bloodlust, cackling dark and crazy at the end of the long ice tunnel, huddled away with her black-windbreakered bodyguards like Colonel Kurtz, with flaming patio torches and the disembodied knees of lesser skaters stuck on poles in her front lawn. She's waiting with the patience of a spider for the day when somebody else's disgrace lifts the black off her name. Then she'll Come Back.

CHAPTER 8

Jump Through the Flaming Tire, Honey . . . Thatta Girl

My little sister was an entrant in a beauty pageant—solely, she assured me, for the scholarship money. I wanted to box her ears, but apparently, while looking through the financial aid lists in her college library, she discovered that, at the time, young white girls looking for help with a liberal arts education were offered little else besides beauty pageants as a means of raising scholarships. Lower-middle- to middle-class American Caucasian chicks are in a not-poor-enough/not-rich-enough financial limbo, and are often compelled, as some form of last resort, to apply for entrance into those laughably demoralizing competitions to determine which girl best acts like an agreeable tub toy. It was something she felt she could walk through without assigning her brain to it; what did she have to do, besides wear a swimsuit, smile, and act stupid?

It has never been a terrific mystery that these contests are completely pornographically revolting and woman-hating on the level of white slavery and foot binding. I was a girlchild in the seventies, and even then, during the peak of their television power, beauty pageants could give a natural human the dark stomach twist. For me, the horror wasn't so much due to the robotish similarities in type and size and hair of the women, but the adolescently fanatical brainwashed quality of all the contestants. These women were clearly in a cult where they were trained to squeal and clap and compete cheerfully for the biggest Pearl Drops smile and autumn mane of hotrolled Breck, and jump for the sardine being dangled off the diving board by some hairy little comedian in a tuxedo. It was obvious to me even as a young girl that the sponsors of such pageants wanted them to be attractive to me; I could tell by the peppy horn-section music and the bright, swirling plastic sets that I was supposed to watch these young women having their pictures shot cuddling with plush Disney animals, singing snazzed-up versions of "It's a Grand Old Flag" and eating rainbow sherbet with glossy lips and preconscious Mormon eroticism, and say, "Ooooooh, I want it, I want the Miss America Barbie doll, I want to tiptoe down the catwalk someday with two dozen long-stems and weep black tears, and I want it because these pert, perfectly pretty girls obviously want it worse than horses or royalty or the Rapture." Who was Miss America supposed to be, anyway, if not an enviable role model for little American girls? Still, I knew it reeked. The smiles were too aggressively wide, the body language too cubist, the enthusiasm too vacuum-packed.

Today, especially in sophisticated urban points on the globe, people tend to laugh about beauty pageants, viewing them as anachronisms that have outlived any real influence they might ever have had, and are now little more than a jokey political eyesore, but the fact remains: the fucking things are STILL THERE, and there's more of them than ever, including JonBenet–style child-beauty contests with redundant names like National All-American USA, Superior Kings and Queens, and Universal Miss & Master International.

In the beauty pageant my sister entered, one of the many entrance hurdles was a questionnaire dotted with insidious Smiley Faces: Are you a Democrat—or a Republican [Smiley Face]? Do you think a *lesbian* should be allowed to be Miss America? Are you Pro-Choice—or Pro-Life [Smiley Face]? It was obvious what the Right Answers were [Smiley Face].

People are easily brainwashed. All you need is some stress, some sleep deprivation, a new language of esoteric terminology, and the constant input of extremist propaganda by the faithful; it's always worked on prisoners of war, hostages, and Scientologists. My sister was amazed by how much she had to appear to *believe* in the world message put forth by the Miss America machine, and frightened at how some of the girls had appeared to effortlessly devour the whole candied fist and call the unnatural pageant manifesto their own. Becoming Miss

America requires an all-out, total fealty to the idea that Miss America isn't just a bunch of pretty girls acting like happily spayed show pets, but a "truly valuable career opportunity" that will "help them" towards becoming doctors and lawyers and other respectable denizens of academia. Plenty of other young women, however, still feel that the pageants are the main thing—the pageant *is* the career goal. They feel that parading around in heels and a swimsuit is a small price to pay in order to get a minor degree of fame for being pretty, and spend their hard-won scholarship money on such educational courses as Weight Training and Pop Singing to help give them an advantage in future pageants.

Miss America is a sexually schizophrenic creature: she is a sex symbol who isn't allowed nipples or her own desire. It is understood by the contestants that in some unwritten law, the queen is supposed to be a virgin. Miss America, when not studying for a career in medicine or its reasonable, humanity-serving equivalent, is supposed to live with her two married and pleasantly aging old parents in a ranch-style house with an American flag in the yard, with a pumpkin on the porch at Halloween and a Christmas tree in the window until January 1. She dotes on her younger siblings and likes ice-skating. She has wonderful orthodontry and a fetching wardrobe that is never too flirty. She is book-smart, but not clever—she never bucks or questions authority. She just happens to be built like a brick whorehouse, but she definitely doesn't acknowledge this fact consciously, or use it with wile. Her cookies are frozen in reserve for her husband, and she's not interested in having one of those any time soon, because her only passion is her "platform" of raising high-school awareness about Muscular Dystrophy. She is preferably a Methodist or Lutheran; any other religion might imply a distastefully passionate feeling for the divine. She likes a Protestant work ethic and wants to help people. Wants to help people. Wants to help People. Beep.

.

The first actual beauty contest, according to unofficial Miss America Pageant history author A. R. Riverol, was for all intents and purposes initiated in 1854 by P. T. Barnum, who was already in the habit of promoting beauty contests for attractive dogs, flowers, and babies. The winners, judged on beauty of face and figure, would win a diamond tiara if married or a dowry chest if unmarried. The contest bombed, however, because the only women who entered were of "questionable reputation."

The first Miss America was crowned in Atlantic City at the "Fall Frolic of 1921," an annual boardwalk event, after being judged "the most beautiful bathing girl in America" by walking around in a "bathing costume" that looked like a large, belted prune with over-the-knee black stockings. Thereafter, the Miss America Pageant, like a B-rate swamp beast, died and kept coming back until 1935, when a woman named Leonora Slaughter helped calcify the pageant into a permanent annual blight. Ms. Slaughter was the initiator of the Miss America Pageant's clenched-fist denial that the pageant is merely a "beauty contest" by introducing corporate-sponsored academic scholarships in 1945. Since then, all Miss Americas have been forced to *appear to believe* in this specious new cheesecake hypocrisy—i.e., the idea that the woman in the swimsuit and heels isn't *really* a woman in a swimsuit and heels (read: hosebag), but a respectable scholar with a bright, morally starched future ahead, being an asset to the community. American television fell quickly in love with this wonderfully flexible means of justifying parading dishy women around in a way everyone secretly knew was dark and tacky, and the little white lie lives on.

When Miss America 1951 refused to pose before the cameras in her swimsuit, Catalina swimwear dissociated from the Miss America Pageant and went on to form the Miss Universe Pageant, thus initiating the creation of sluttier-than-thou offshoots of the Miss America Pageant. This pageant and those that followed opted to cut out the hypocritical "scholarship" focus and go, unapologetically, straight for the T&A.

The late sixties brought Miss America a flurry of girdle-burnings and protests by the National Organization for Women, but to no avail—the pageant carried on, with a seemingly inexhaustible supply of guileless, peach-faced muffets and leggy Uncle Toms willing to sell out the bra-less feminist sisterhood in order to mince around the stage in paneled swimsuits and get their pictures taken. The protests stopped, and Miss America kept going, more televised than ever before.

A Massive Swelling

In 1983, the first black Miss America, Vanessa ("the Undressa") Williams, was forced to resign from her post after being featured not once but *twice* in *Penthouse* magazine, in black-and-white lesbian art photos and full leather-'n'-handcuffs sadomasochistic gear, respectively. Miss Williams went on to be the only Miss America ever to be truly famous or widely beloved by the American masses, or to have any kind of real career in the entertainment industry. The irony of her forced resignation was most succinctly encapsulated in *The Onion: Our Dumb Century* with the headline VANESSA WILLIAMS TARNISHES MISS AMERICA CROWN WITH SEXIST OBJECTIFICATION.

Lately, America's women's movements seem to have lolled over like a punctured dirigible, letting the shows go on unfettered by any kind of negative backlash. Many women have given in to a live-and-let-live attitude: if some women work that hard to achieve that ridiculous bimbo-showpiece variety of attractiveness, they must desperately *want* to be objectified, so why stop them?

I believe we have to look at the pageants differently; in an era where there is glossy pornography available for every conceivable flavor of perversion, swimsuits aren't a serious threat. It's the mindset that turns my heart black; the aggressively kiss-ass, corporate-conformist cheerleading that makes the girls win that gives me the danger chills.

My sister, a diminutive brunette, was momentarily brainwashed by the pageant she was in. She was so taken in by the whole theory that the judges were basing their decisions on talent and personality, etc., that she was actually surprised and kind of crushed when a six-foot idiot blonde with no talent and huge tits won. It hurt her feelings. Then one of the pageant runners, as consolation, smilingly told her she needed to lose a few pounds. The veil of respectability lifted suddenly off the pageant with a rude jerk, exposing the billboard-sized beaver shot within.

The one way that the Miss America Pageant seems to backwardly apologize for itself is its recent rash of shamelessly soppy political correctness, e.g., the recent crowning of a deaf Miss America. This move appeals to the tragedy-loving section of America who adore *Reader's Digest* articles about the bravery of Christopher Reeve and support the breeding of legless and dwarfy "Twisty" cats, because their struggle for normal movement is so "inspirational." I think that there should be a wholly separate beauty-format contest for women of "Brave and Saintly" status, which should include not only the handicapped but also the merely ballsy, with activities that include Pulling a Rubber Orphan from a Burning Tenement, Refusing to Give Away Political Secrets Under Torture, the Liberty Climb for paraplegics, during which women without the use of their legs climb the stairs to the torch of the Statue of Liberty unassisted, and a talent segment during which the women tear their skirts into ribbons and tie excellent tourniquets, and paint gorgeous landscapes in oil with their teeth. This contest could be significantly less demeaning than one that pitted young women's bodies against one another in bikinis; this would be an "inner beauty contest" that celebrates true greatness in the crippled and homely. It's right not to confuse the porn with the principle.

International beauty pageants have really gotten a shock since South America went off the women-are-three-holed-chattel scale of human reason. A huge number of women in Argentina are now getting state-funded cosmetic plastic surgery, because they are allowed to argue that without a certain standard of conventional beauty, they are unemployable. Venezuela has long been famous for its beauty-queen boot camps, where dusky, voluptuous Latin girls are chemically and surgically stretched and dyed into carcinogenic blondes with ribless waists and throbbing Evita-style lusts for social domination. They are the only women with any kind of tangible power in South America, and supermodels are still the highest-paid women in the world, and the same things go on in every country everywhere, in one form or another.

The free world turns on a gravitational axis of sex and money, and most women are so frightened about not getting enough of either one that they're all fucked into self-loathing, self-defacing kibble. Much lip service is paid to the "We've Come a Long Way, Baby" improved collective state of women, but we're still, as the Lennon/Ono team so violently put it, the niggers of the world, and one of the biggest problems is still the blow-dried Stepford zombies in the American-flag bathing suits and the high white pumps, starving and tottering out into the hot lights, smiling and wagging their tails.

Women have always been the worst enemies of women. It's always the grandmothers who hold down screaming little girls for the clitorectemy razor; there's always some fetching bottle-blonde like Pam Anderson whose super-commercially wanton presence alone is enough to scare insecure women into getting their faces and breasts cut open with little knives; and it's beauty-pageant contestants who year after year swallow the same wiggling mouthful of elderly sex politics and allow there to be more beauty pageants. Until the bad spirit that compels those young women is beaten out of them, everyone may as well head for Argentina, because it's just going to get worse and worse. Soon, something along the lines of a Miss Hot California Pageant should be slithering down the chrome pole onto our televisions, wearing nothing but oil and wet string. Groups of little girls will be getting perianal Brazilian wax jobs on their thirteenth birthdays and new tits for freshman year. Even Barbie won't be secure anymore; they'll have to remove part of her tawny, hinged ass and inject it into her hollow face before she can feel right in a thong.

Miss America needs to be given a proper burial; she needs to be allegorically gang-raped on a pool table by a bunch of Portuguese longshoremen and left out in an alley to die. Then her face, a composite of all Miss Americas in the past, will be vulcanized into a Betty

Crocker–type trademark and placed on collector remembrance plates. She will be denatured and sterile, smiling in a tiara from the porcelain, just like Princess Di, a consumer symbol of something past and pretty and unreal; someone's dangerously naïve idea of feminine success a long, long, time ago.

PART THREE

L.A. Is My Lady

CHAPTER 9

As a Dog Returneth
to Its Own Vomit,
So Doth L.A.

Does not this town steam with the fumes of slaughtered spirit?
Don't you see the soul hanging like a limp, dirty rag? And they
still make newspapers of these rags!
— FRIEDRICH NIETZSCHE,
Thus Spake Zarathustra

*B*ack in '95, I thought: In the last half-decade of the
century, one must stick both barrels of Armageddon
fearlessly in one's mouth and live in the Fuselage of
Human Error, which is surely Los Angeles.

I relocated to Hollywood in order to be closer to the
doom and failure of the collective human soul over
the power of Evil, which is most succinctly displayed in
the workings of Hollywood. What better place to go than
a city that orchestrates all of the attitudes I hate the most

about the American mentality? What better place to experience career angst, rage, and disappointment than a
city where women dress like prostitutes and speak like
babies and men are pornography addicts and are aloof
and comfortable in their self-loathing and unrepentant
cash-sucking? I thought I would fiddle like Nero with my
nourishing little artistic pursuits while Babylon burned.
I thought of Mary Baker Eddy, founder of Christian
Science, jotting down the spiritual-healing formulas of
Science and Health in her attic room while all around her
barbaric medicinal practices punctured and leached the
last dregs of life out of the sick. I will fight my own tiny
crusade, I thought, I will be a blot of golden reason in a
landscape of moral decay.

The "Ha-ha, Satan lives in L.A." jokes are not really
funny anymore, because they're too eerily true. There's
so many hoof tracks and triple-6 brands on the teats of the
locals that the presence of Real Evil is as banal and commonplace as that of a Big Mac. L.A. is the place where
Satan squats with an enormous ladle and dips deeply into
his black cavity to extract huge soiled wads of cash, which
he then pitches at the heads of the inhabitants below
with such speed and force that they are rendered first unconscious, then punchy and depressed. This affliction
causes them to overfeed the Dark Lord a-more with their
incessant compromises in the workplace, and He devours
and digests their creepy and self-negating decisions by
day, and befouls them anew with the sooty issue of their
moral failures each evening. Los Angeles brings to mind
all of the jokes everyone tells about lawyers. If major

cities had human personalities, L.A. would be either an entertainment management executive or a defense attorney, in a red plastic economy Mercedes, driving twenty miles an hour on the 10 Santa Monica, getting a hand job from a seventeen-year-old prostitute while lying to his wife on the cell phone. The rhythm of the streets of L.A. is the soundtrack of *Faust* performed by Yanni and John Tesh, and it sells zillions and zillions of copies.

■

If Hollywood has been intrinsically corrupt since its inception, it is exponentially more so now. L.A. today is a sad and damaging fiasco, a far cry from the champagne star giddiness of the thirties, when a beautiful girl could hit the Big Time by walking into a soda fountain with no socks. Now there is no counting the miles of hotel sheets a would-be starlet will have to swim through to get a reading for a walk-on part in a sitcom, or the horrible court battles a wannabe jukebox hero will have to endure before he can wrench his own music out of the gnarled grip of insidious bloodsucking industry trolls, or the endless hall of mirrors anybody who wants to work in film will have to break her nose against before she can be a personal boot-wiper for "important people." Everyone in L.A. walks around with the noxious smog impregnated down into the entrails of his/her being. Everyone KNOWS it's corrupt, all of it. It's the Mexican prison of art: Everything is controlled by money and the twisted whims of a few fat guys holding the keys. But it's the only game in town, and if you're not playing, God help you, you may as well try to get a job with the illegal aliens down at El Pollo Loco.

■

Incredibly talented people, marvelous artists, come to L.A. because they believe that the life-affirming purity of their talent and ability will blaze a righteous and heroic path to the gleaming halls of Deserved Fortune. Many Sensitive Actors and Writers flocking to Hollywood consider themselves to be aesthetic priests, living as they imagine nineteenth-century actors or opera singers lived, and dedicating their lives to art through faith and discipline. They picture their life in the lively arts as lilac-bedecked high teas in tailored pantaloons with the Cultured and Royal, majestically quoting Eleonora Duse and riding around in bucket-shaped vintage touring cars crowing Gilbert and Sullivan with blond locks and silky foulards floating behind them like misplaced namby ponces from *Brideshead Revisited*. The squalor of the actual show-biz industry then shocks them into a gibbering and shaking state of posttraumatic stress that leaves them conversationally capable of little more than dry heaves.

They eventually discover that the sinister realities of Hollywood are far worse than the casting-couch horror fantasies of being slipped date-rape mickeys by hair-covered old executive brutes. Poverty and disillusionment set in, and their belief in themselves is chipped away little by little, and eventually, out of starvation or a corrosion of integrity, they compromise themselves utterly, and actually *audition* for roles on MTV beach-volleyball/daytime masturbation comedies where artistes of their delicate temperaments are beaten like piñatas by women with large teeth and rubber breasts. Their agents then devise "reels" of these atrocities, which ensure their future pigeonholing in the most unholy, hair-peelingly idiotic television roles imaginable. It is nearly impossible to be a working artist in L.A. without singing for Salad Shooters or romancing Dobermans for Cinemax or writing jingles for Pizza Nuggets or pilot scripts for Jim Belushi. Finally, everyone is neutered by the jaws of the omnivorous Moloch "Format," which all industry drones are terrified to unchain themselves from, and in the end the last pathetic shreds of everyone's creativity are assassinated. Then everybody has lunch.

∎

Most L.A. "meetings" are more depressing and pointless than going out and meeting the daughter of a friend of your mom's. There is no real reason for either party to be in the room; both want something they secretly know the other person isn't going to provide.

This is the typical Meet & Greet experience:

You walk into the reception hall of the movie studio, which is covered with the posters of whatever unwatchable films the company has done in the past few years, invariably sequels of everything you've ever gagged over at the video store: *I Spit on Your Grave III; Cornbread, Earl & Me Too; I'm Still Dancing as Fast as I Can; Bert Rigby You're a Fool II;* and anything with some benign family robot.

"So! Tell us a little about yourself!" is the first question the Hollywood Person asks you. This is code for "I have no idea who you are, and I haven't read anything your agent has sent me." Once you have mumbled through your demoralizing tap solo and shown them your teeth, they roll into the "Now I should probably tell you a little about what We do" monologue, which they have down to the economical, pure-information level of a telemarketing pitch.

This speech tells you which ingenious Big Star (e.g., Loni Anderson, Suzanne Somers, Alyssa Milano) is the creative figurehead of the company, and that he or she, the speaker, is one of nine or ten impotent executives who can't do anything without the approval of nine or ten other executives and/or the elusive approval of the invisible star, who is making a wonderful children's film right now about a cyborg killer whale with ESP in Tahiti.

"So what's *next* for you?" is generally the wind-up question. Translation: "Are you going to be famous next year? Because if you aren't, what you have been pitching me is so totally unmarketable, you may as well be trying to sell me some reprint of a fiction article from Spanish *Hustler.*"

You then pull out your parking ticket for validation. The meeting is over. They go on to have fourteen more meetings like that this week, during which absolutely nothing happens. So do you.

■

There's a big luscious peach of a dream in L.A. The peach has been repeatedly exposed as overripe and tainted with

wormholes left by the seedily tragic realities of M. Monroe and J. Dean and R. Phoenix and *The Day of the Locust*,
but it's still the only giant peach in town. Even if it's
wet-brown and crawling with centipedes, everyone wants
their bite. There's plenty of folks who haven't gotten a
real taste of the thing that will tell you how lousy it is, but
under all of the sour grapes, everybody still feels, deeply,
that Celebrity is the ultimate brass ring. They may hate
Fame for ignoring and humiliating them, they may hate
themselves for being addicted to that humiliation; they
may know Fame will destroy them and know just as
surely that they want to be destroyed worse than they
want True Love, and they may loudly malign the Bubble
of Fame for turning people into overstimulated plastic
robo-whores, but deep inside, they still believe in the
twisted magic of it all. Fame is still held by L.A. folk and
most other Americans to be the only thing that can truly
validate a human life.

■

In L.A. everyone blows gold up your ass with tremendous
sincerity. When you first get to L.A., you think, "Wow,
everyone here APPRECIATES me so much as an artist . . .
they really GET IT here." After the first two weeks you
realize that this is a huge lie. The reality is, everyone in
L.A. spews mendacity with reckless desperation: i.e., "I
don't care if I really personally hate you, you can be the
most frighteningly power-mad cannibal since Idi Amin,
but if you are the next Tom Arnold I will lay you down on
a buttery divan and gleefully suck all the snot out of your

head." This totally counterintuitive policy of indiscriminate sycophantism seems to work for all the working L.A.
industry people, with little argument and a lot of self-
flagellation.

In a similarly morally zombified way, if a person actually becomes famous, they are somehow ethically exempt
from acceptable human conduct, and nobody, due to
some grave universal error, is allowed to say anything
when they step outrageously out of line. An acrobat
friend of mine we'll call Sparky was hanging out with a
very famous heavyweight actor, doing what Hollywood
people do: drinking heavily and hanging around at three
A.M. Being Themselves. Sparky has a proclivity towards
wearing very large plastic children's watches from Korea,
with big cartoon heads, etc. The actor politely asked
to see the watch, and Sparky obliged, unstrapping the
Velcro animal and handing it over. The actor put the
watch on the coffee table, pulled a .45 that had been concealed in his pants, and shot it, the incredible blast terrifying everyone in the living room into a sickly green
silence. The actor started smirking, in his trademark
multiplex fashion. To dispel the vapor of unsafe and terrible feeling that pervaded the room, another guest
drawled, "Hey, Sparky, now why don't you give him your
necklace." Everybody chuckled with blood-sweating re-
lief, and the evening went on. The actor never apologized,
Sparky bought himself a new watch, and the incident became just another laughable, aura-enhancing, iconic legend of how that star is such a bitchin' psycho.

A Massive Swelling

■

The industry action in L.A. is all about being a part of a particular tidepool. Once you're in the game, you're in, everybody knows you and your particular strengths and weaknesses, and you get passed from hand to hand like a party joint. All of the "employed" industry people that I know—actors, key grips, wardrobe personnel, development executives, etc.—have the same attitude about working in "the Business" that one gets in the middle of a particularly debilitating acid trip: just let go of the wheel and roll with it, don't say no to anything, don't blow any of your connections, and opportunities will come your way that lead you down the wet silicone rabbit hole. In this way, you will witness all of the shame and horror and wild luck and deathly euphoria that comes from running alongside unabashed avarice and total moral nonchalance, every day.

■

Successful behind-the-scenes players in Hollywood— i.e., those who have held their desk jobs long enough to be lulled into an impression (false) of security—generally become pampered gargoyles in loyal service to the most hateful machinery of skullfucking artistic compromise. A friend—we shall call her Madeline—wrote for a little-known syndicated sitcom. The producer—"Buck"—is someone who has been sustaining a steady stream of schlock TV successes since the seventies. The system works for Buck. He invited us to his house for a private screening of a movie, the style of which he wanted Madeline to emulate when writing the sitcom.

As Madeline and I drove up through the Emerald City–like gate to the private driveway, I had an overwhelming realization: Buck was sick rich like nobody I'd ever seen before. I felt like one of the nuns who vomited when witnessing the disparity between the Papa Doc Duvalier palace and the mud shacks of the Haitian poor. It turned out Buck's house was formerly owned by a shirtless titty-man actor from the 1950s. All of the architecture reflected that tract-homey, Brady Bunch Polynesian aesthetic reminiscent of patio torches and indoor wet bars and ice cubes molded into torsos of naked ladies, except everything was preposterously huge and expensive. There was a palm-studded island sculpted out of textured cement around the ultra-blue waters of Buck's vast, many-laned, cloverleaf-interchange-esque swimming arena. You could almost see the ghostly echoes of past poolside action in your third eye: women with thirteen-inch waists in vinyl G-strings and breasts the size of speaker cabinets discussing pilot options, outrageously bombed on hunger and Chardonnay and vitamin B and the kind of screaming pink self-loathing that burns supersonically through all psyches in L.A. like a dated racing stripe.

Buck himself was a pleasant patriarch-tycoon in action slacks, with thirteen children from five marriages and an eighty-nine-pound wife who couldn't have been more obviously bulimic if she had had a plastic visor on her head that said BULIMIC in big block letters that lit up. She offered us king-sized Kit Kat bars and ice cream. The wife was fluorescent with a howling need to be looked in the eye with love or understanding or something, a starving ghost suffering like a friendless autocrat in the Hollywood Hills.

The living room was a gray-carpeted football field studded with vibrating leather couches. Madeline and I began the slow shuddering which was to accompany us through the rest of the evening, particularly when the personal twenty-by-twelve-foot 35mm movie screen dropped out of a subtly placed electronic door in the ceiling. The movie, some melodramatic foreign thriller, had moments of manipulative knee-jerk-emotional Spielbergism and obviousness that made Madeline and me clutch at each other's thighs and bite halfway through our tongues trying not to groan like we'd been poisoned. Without fail, every time one of these icky violin-and-moist-eyed-lens scenes appeared, Buck would pipe up and say, "THIS! This here! This is beautiful. Can you write like this?" His sentimental hack vision of "drama" slimed over us like artificial butter flavoring.

Madeline was a wonderful writer at the mercy of an insipid tyrant, who is still able to successfully impose his ideas about art throughout his kingdom because he knows where the rich blood is in the deep pulse of American tastelessness. The work, despite the money, was a great deal more demoralizing than working in a car wash, where a little ingenuity will at least get you a pat on the back or a tip. Madeline's better ideas, needless to say, were never used, and she eventually became so ashamed of the work that she began working under a pseudonym and subcontracting the work to untrained friends who needed the money. Buck never noticed.

While Buck enjoys his ill-gotten Valhalla in the hills and a complete divorce from reality, reality in L.A. gets poorer, weirder, and worse.

There are a few hair-raising quality-of-life issues in Los Angeles, such as the fact that attitudes towards racism, instead of getting more enlightened with education and time, are rampantly degenerating—a retrogression completely supported and for all intents and purposes whipped further backwards by the torch holders of Hollywood status quo. Racism, which you don't see an obvious lot of in more-or-less-successfully integrated cities like San Francisco, is a whole different ball game in L.A., where the African-Americans have grown up on such a completely different planet—e.g., Compton—that they get treated like radioactive werewolves by most white L.A. residents. The black radio station advertisements are so exclusively Ebonic, they are like listening to a Smithsonian folk recording from the Deep South in the thirties: "I ain't trustin' my tax refun' check wit' nobody but the Imperial No-ID check-cashin' center, 'cause I wants ALL my money, honey!" The ads are all written in black urban patois with a "sho 'nuff" creepy throwback style that celebrates the kind of grammatical ignorance and negative fried-chicken stereotyping that would make any black college student cry with frustration. The rash of straight-out-da-ghetto films a few years ago, and the rising superpopularity of *COPS* and *Real-Life Horrible Shit Happening to Criminals*–type shows just goes to show you that our depraved American penal system no longer just provides cages to storehouse and hide those (brown) persons economically disenfranchised from the capitalist system as a whole, but now also offers a rich and boundless source of prurient entertainment. As the quality of education in the U.S. plummets, inversely doth the morbid interest in other people's desperation rise: ignorant, small-eyed, angry people screaming and clobbering each other is the lucrative fruit of daytime television. Deep Personal Disgrace has replaced biography in the *This Is Your Life*–type voyeuristic television format. The "contestants" are reduced to the simplest and most damning happenstance that perverted them into a spectacle of disdain—e.g., show captions like BITCH, YOU UGLY or HOW HARD WOULD YOU BITE YOUR TODDLER FOR $10,000? The natural end zone of depravity, prisons, I fear will become our new televised Roman Colosseum, and black men the new dancing bears, led around by the septum and kept on the mambo foot-chart with mace and stun guns.

As racism quietly ascends to crisis proportions, so does sexism. L.A. has blue laws censoring references to pornography in the media, which means that nobody can talk about or advertise what apparently everybody is doing. From what I experienced, average porno consumption in L.A. seemed drastically increased from what it was in Northern California. Nearly all the men, young and older, that I met in L.A. openly kept *Club International*s and *Penthouse*s around the house in stacks as high as their neck, dating back to the seventies, with dog-eared "favorite" shaved-crotch shots that they treated with the tenderness of old friends. Male Lip Service to Belief in Feminism vs. Male Desire of the Basest Forms of Feminine Exploitation is a big conundrum in L.A. One is left with the overall impression that most men in L.A. are so disgusted and confused by their own tacky sexual peccadilloes that they simply bury themselves in mounds of vice, and instead of eschewing the depravity of porn, try to embrace the normalness of it by having it be as much an obvious part of their lives as cigars or Wellbutrin.

Various entertainment institutions seem to be directly responsible for the widespread acceptability of L.A.'s happy porn addiction: old-school standup comedy, for example, in its original incarnation of being indelibly linked to strip clubs, seems to have sown a lot of enduring cheap boobie laffs, like the eighties proliferation of frat-boy jack-off comedies personified by *Porky's*. The Erotic Thriller genre, in which a beautiful woman trapped in a web of intrigue is at some point obliged to be chainsawed in half while massaging her breasts in the shower, is another big porn-desensitizer.

Fashion and entertainment-industry magazines are the little sisters of porn, and any actress or female singer/ songwriter worth her weight in money is going to appear shirtless with her hands over her nipples or doggie-style in lingerie on the cover of something. The women-being-naked-as-a-form-of-"empowerment" question remains a very sticky issue; as Larry Flynt said, "Whoever controls the pussy controls the planet," but what do such photos actually get the women, besides a crusty white stain on their glossy graven images? Has a *Playboy* centerfold or a *Maxim* layout or any nudie stroke-shot ever really boosted anyone's career? LaToya? Demi? Elle Macpherson? Dana Plato? Empowered?

Farrah Fawcett was a grave example of this misstep, having made a very tottery, self-humiliating veer into the nether realm of scronky withered nudism and lite-porn layouts, apparently fueled by some kind of terrible chemical secret. Farrah chucked over years' worth of respectable TV workability to careen into a rut that even ancient porn stars like Porsche Lynn wouldn't stoop to—i.e., becoming the type of sprawling, nondiscriminating succubus commonly found on curling and brown calendars over the toolbox of the neighborhood transmission specialist. There is no fecundity wafting off the page in an airbrushed *Playboy* shot of debased old Farrah, whose once-comestible sexiness was quietly beaten to death by Ryan O'Neal in the eighties. Poor decisions like these are made when a star's personality begins to sag: Farrah lost the Swerve, the elusive lust-magic that led celebrity to her door in the first place, and it clearly drove her nuts.

Hollywood must, of course, give the public what it wants, regardless of how vile it might be. The makers of these gruesome popular works rationalize their greed-basted, misogynistic production, because they are richly rewarded for pandering to these low consumer instincts. These "Who am I to judge?" executive-producing humanitarians are deep in the lifeblood of L.A.—a viral opportunism that only kills common decency. Hollywood, as a purveyor of "entertainment," is more or less the equivalent of the corner store in the ghetto that primarily sells Wild Irish Rose to homeless alcoholics and menthol cigarettes to eighth-graders. If they don't sell it, somebody else will.

Many ambitious Hollywood pragmatists have wholly embraced the sex angle to launching virtually any kind of career, sailing clear over any pretense of propriety or legitimacy and diving directly into the hardcore pussy-sell.

A well-known musician friend of mine was scheduled to have a meeting with some new female singer/songwriter whose upcoming record he was being asked to contribute to. The singer, a red-mouthed alternative chippy, came over to his house with a cheap boom box in a tennis skirt and no underwear, sat down with her legs spread, and started grinding out her favorite number on his couch. He was badly shaken and mortified, and refused the gig. Six months later, the song was a Top Ten Hit, several other musicians having enjoyed the singer/songwriter's flexible methods of collaboration.

What men routinely get away with in L.A. would get the tips of their noses sliced off in most of the social channels in New York. Women are different in New York; their methods of womanly operation are different from those in Southern California: more brains, more independent wealth, less sexual Uncle Tomming. New York women look at L.A. women with the same head-shaking dismay with which L.A. women regard beauty-pageant contestants.

"Whadda ROCK!" I once shouted in the champagne din as I artlessly struck up conversation with a plastic-surgery-enhanced lady at a New York premiere party. I was noticing the gem-shaped ice sculpture she had on her ring finger, big as a shoebox.

"THANKS!" she trumpeted back, packed tight in her red bolero jacket with the little Chanels down the front. "I'm WORTH it!" she blared. "GODDAMMIT, IT'S TRUE!"

I admired her belligerent confidence. In L.A., had I screamed "Whadda ROCK!" at somebody, it probably would have been some kind of thirtysomething Bo Derek type paralyzed by the impositions of being Good-Looking and scrambling with every cell of her being to retain this status. She would have mumbled something inaudible and shivered away from me and thought me crass, even though she would have sucked every knob in town to have gotten to the party in the first place. She would look at me like I reminded her of where she came from, some lower-middle-class pit of terminal mediocrity and nonglamour that she inflated her breasts to enormous size to float far away from. L.A. women all strangle themselves to stay the prescribed porno-rag version of "beautiful," so that they can marry somebody and get Power. In New York, women are proud tyrants in their own right and go straight for the Power themselves and leave the beauty race to nine-foot, sixty-three-pound teenage mutant supermodels like Kirsty Hume, who is as much a freak of nature as a three-headed praying mantis, and everybody knows this and feels OK about eating.

■

What the men in L.A. seem to want in a woman is a wildly compassionate psychologist/nymphomaniac who wears very severe minisuits in the daytime and rips them open at night to reveal a garment made of rubber and steel hooks. The ideal woman has a six-digit income, the body of a Japanese chrome sex robot, and a great sense of humor, and isn't all hung up on this ugly overblown thing of being "objectified." The men of L.A. leap around like amphetamine-psychotic satyrs driven mad by depression and seek sex with anybody, drink and drive and *not* drink and drive with equal lack of composure, and worry bleeding holes in themselves about not being enough of a "Player." Power = Sex. Power is the sexiest thing in town, and likewise, one must be sexy to have true Hollywood Power. Hollywood implicitly states: If you would look wrong in bed with Jennifer Aniston, you may as well have your feet pierced and be left on some remote desert hill to be Exposed, and thus avoid embarrassment for everybody. Let the twenty-year-olds run the planet, and give the bleached old bones of the discarded elders to Native

Americans so they can make designer lamps for the Sundance catalog.

■

Ironically, leading men's nipples are just as exploited as women's nipples in the City of Angels. When Brad Pitt and his pouty-lipped soft-focus sex-boy shot appeared on the cover of *Vanity Fair* at the peak of his box-office domination a few years ago, and he gave that fantastically vapid interview, it dawned on me: He doesn't even know what's being done to him, he doesn't know how sarcastic Annie Leibovitz's photos of him are, he doesn't know he's being groomed to be Hollywood's pumping-buttock gigolo boy until he's too old to fit the bill. They plucked and waxed him into a cartoon of blowzy supermarket masculinity; they dressed him in a big white pirate shirt, the male version of a thong, and primed him to simulate intercourse with every female in Hollywood until his hair gets thin and his dance card gets thrown away. There are sure to be plenty of spike-heel and wing-tip tracks all over his face and private areas by the time that piece of wet cardboard hits the floor.

But Brad soaks up the biggest attention and loves it, in spurts, getting photographed for *W* facedown on a concrete floor with his pants around his knees for those who fantasize about homosexual prison rape. Brad enjoys the power of his own objectification like a drunk girl whipping her bra off in a nightclub, all the while looking like he owns his own physical self less than a preteen kidnapped by Turkish pimps. There are countless numbers of death-wish hitchhikers by the side of that yellow brick road who would suck anything out of anywhere for a chance to take his place.

■

"Americans love junk," said George Santayana. "It's not the junk that bothers me; it's the love." L.A. is the royal culmination of all junk. Everyone—rich, poor, black, white, man, woman—all of them debasing themselves and each other in a torrid network of abusive codependence, everyone hypnotized and enslaved by the Big Project: i.e., the absolute worst and smarmiest fucked-up human impulses distilled into film and video, for billions and billions.

■

My present attitude towards Hollywood is that we should impose no limitations on it whatsoever, and let it get as sick and filthy and blood-drunk as it can possibly get. Perhaps when Americans are exhausted by blatant moral ruin, there will be more movement towards true creative light. "Let all the poisons that lurk in the mud hatch out," mumbled Derek Jacobi in *I, Claudius,* when he realized that only a grand sabotage of Rome's Imperial structure would bring about a return to the Roman Republic. O Vengeful Gods, bring on the Toads! Bring on the Locusts and the Wormwood! Let blood run down Santa Monica Boulevard and the Dead of Forest Lawn rise from their compact little graves and roam in bitter agony down the Sunset Strip. Let the rich and famous eat the firstborn sons of the Common Man. Only then will the insidious disease of Hollywood be reckoned with as the soul-killing beast it truly is. Only then will we know to bomb everything west of the San Andreas fault and south of Bakersfield into gravel and let it sift into the sea.

The Pacific, however, does not deserve such pollution.

CHAPTER 10

Crossing Boundaries: Towards a New Hermeneutics of Dumb Pimps Like Bruce Willis

*T*here is a line at the end of *Willy Wonka and the Chocolate Factory* where Gene Wilder is flying Charlie and Jack Albertson over the city in the glass elevator, and Willy says, "You know what happened to the little boy who suddenly got everything he ever wanted, don't you, Charlie?" and Charlie asks, "No, what?" and Willy says, "He lived happily ever after," and the two of them embrace and that beautiful song swells (". . . woooorld, of pure imagination . . .") and everybody cries because little Charlie deserved it all and he got it and it's magic.

In Hollywood there are a whole lot of little boys and girls who got everything they always wanted, but there are very few of them who everyone agrees really deserved it. And are they living happily ever after? It is presumed that they should be. What the hell right have they not to be?

Stars, to bowdlerize Fitzgerald, are not like you and me. They have many more snarling communication problems with the world, and it shows in their eyes like a hematoma. Many stars are so Not of This Earth Anymore that they are just bad crazy and eccentric to the point of not being fun ever again, and everyone but their entourage listens to their self-referential babbling with wide-open looks of total confusion on their faces, while their inner circle of handlers all laugh and say, "God, that's GREAT!! Ha ha ha," with such convincing enthusiasm that it almost seems understandable that they make all that money. To people outside their cash circle of immediate "friends," stars look a bit like declawed zoo animals who've been mollycoddled for so long they don't look wild anymore, just kind of sick and decorative in an unwholesome way, because all their meat is brought to them boneless in clean white buckets and they bat the tetherball around and don't do anything befitting a real animal anymore. Many stars don't do much that is befitting of a real human anymore, unless their nannies are sick and they are forced to tend to their own offspring themselves. Most veer into perverse self-indulgence, and tailspin into either unregenerate after-hours nightclubbing with models or "eccentric" and "artistic" behavior, which generally consists of random and abusive tantrums

towards those they perceive as inferiors and/or brandish-
ing handguns.

Most celebrities suffer from an advanced strain of
Hubris, which leads them to believe that everything they
do is cute and interesting. These stars believe that they
are well-rounded, Renaissance-style "artists" and are capable of doing more than the thing that they originally
gained success for—i.e.: Actors start thinking they can
sing, or write, or direct. Models start thinking they can act,
or sing. Authors and songwriters start thinking they can
paint. Once in a great while, we will be surprised by the
versatility of a talent, but most of the time we are hushed
into a helpless viewing of an enormous ego performing far
outside of its element, flailing grotesquely, wrongly and
shamelessly. We shall call the unfortunate disease that
compels a star to disgrace itself with an unbecoming art
medium "Brunitis," lovingly named after Bruce Willis's
blues album debut, *The Return of Bruno,* which left us all
paralyzed with feelings of hopelessness and despair.

Music seems to be a particular lure for those afflicted
with a terrifyingly optimistic sense of self. Take, for example, the irony-free singing careers of Bruce Willis, Jennifer
Lopez, Cybill Shepherd, Eddie Murphy, Kevin Bacon,
David Hasselhoff, Anthony Michael Hall, and others.
These aspiring crooners want to sing, so they get a big
glossy shot of their heads on the cover of a CD and belt
out gummy, beige versions of pop music or puerile renditions of classic standards in a taking-the-karaoke-
too-seriously kind of way. I was once forced to witness a
horrifying example of morbid Brunitis when I was taken

to a small blues bar to see derelict actor Harry Dean Stanton sing in the New Year. When we entered the bar, Harry, already suffering "spins," was using the microphone stand as a means to remain standing. "Harry needs another cocktail!" someone from the stage would yell every few minutes, as Harry unintelligibly moaned like he was passing kidney stones to "Wooly Bully" in cryptic and fluctuating time signatures which the musicians tried to follow, with the maddening futility of someone trying to grasp a dollar bill twisting away in a strong breeze. At one point Harry lurched off the stage mid-song and began shuffling around the bar, fumbling cardboard hats onto the heads of fearful young women, his dirty thumbs slipping into their eyes. "Harry's going to hand out hats now, heh heh," chortled the bandleader, treating the alcohol-poisoned actor as if he were a charming Down syndrome child. Any man in that bar with a loving heart would have beaten Harry out cold with a pool cue and dragged him off to sleep in someone's car. Instead, the crowd, somehow inured to these ghastly spectacles, clapped, and laughed, and whistled. What would be considered pathetically unsocialized, crisis-level behavior in normal people is lovably eccentric for Harry Dean Stanton, movie star.

Dogstar, the band of Keanu Reeves, was one of the saddest "musical" experiences I was ever privy to. Keanu, aspiring recording artist, may have some kind of "star" magic, he may be a beautiful poster boy; but strap a guitar to his body and he becomes suddenly concave, charmless and invisible, a conduit of nothing but pain. Even the chubby, nylon-minidressed teen groupies in black lipliner and strappy white platforms who came exclusively to scream and cry and hopefully be molested, who crammed each other flat at the front of the stage for the closest glimpse of Keanu, couldn't quite get up the enthusiasm to scream anymore after the third song. By the time the Dogstar set was winding to a close with a cover of Neil Young's "Keep on Rocking in the Free World," many of the frosted little girls had painfully trudged in their too-high stilt shoes to the back of the auditorium, where they were using their baby-fat charm to beg the bartenders to secretly let them have beer. Keanu's humility was not false as he sulked offstage, head down, to a polite smattering of walk-off applause. The lights in the auditorium went quickly up; the house music boomed in before the rest of the band was able to scuttle off in retreat. Nobody wanted to see Keanu not get an encore, and be even sadder, so they didn't even give him the opportunity.

Does our love for famous people extend to the point that we, their adoring fans, must patiently watch them as they interrupt the grown-up party like spoiled children demanding that we watch them perform a graceless somersault on the rug? The inner sanctum of suckers-up around these people apparently does not tell the Brunitis-stricken celebrities that they are teetering horribly on the abyss of Appalling Shame, but merely insists that the offending album will go over great in Europe and Japan. All energy is channeled towards protecting the fragile Star Psyche, all the while merrily disregarding and smiling in denial over the devastating consequences of giving the celeb unbridled encouragement. After all, the gargantuan aura of a celebrity is the commodifiable aspect of the celebrity, and it is the job of the mendacious entourage to fluff and blow the star's aura into a constant, humming erection, regardless of whether or not the aura is in desperately bad taste.

■

Stars worry about being recognized and bothered by the charismatically collapsed human filth who want to invade their aura-world. After you see a few stars on the street, you realize that they are generally very, very tiny people, with enormous heads, in roughly the proportions of a Charms Blow Pop. The additive light from the big screen invariably pumps their personal energies out concentrically to President or Jesus level, that which gives them the illusion of height on camera also giving them delusional ideas of who they are and what they are capable of in their actual lives. Stars seethe with an "I really wish I was just a person, like you" vibration, which is sandwiched by an "I'm really actually better than you" tinge, which is tied together by a contrail of loathing which is of the "I kind of hate myself for thinking I'm kind of better than you" essence, which is surrounded by a "The fact

that I kind of hate myself for thinking I'm better than you
proves how superior I truly am" thing. The real spiritual
masters among the stars are said to have a fifth concentric
aura that goes back to self-hatred again, but few have
ever seen it.

■

Some stars have a Brunitis-tinged bent towards pontificat-
ing on spiritual matters, and quickly find a way to reason
that their popular terrestrial superpowers are the direct result of extraterrestrial superiority: i.e., they are so materi-
ally fortunate here on earth because in a higher realm,
they are of tremendous metaphysical importance, and God
loves them better than everyone else. Michael Jackson has
clearly flopped over into a full-blown Messiah Complex
and thinks he is a Jesus. Madonna likes to give karmic ad-
vice. Richard Gere hangs out with the Dalai Lama and
lends his majestic, spiritually attuned speaking voice to
various Buddhist audiotapes. Tom Cruise and Nicole
Kidman and John Travolta all suffer from the hawk-eyed
ultra-smugness that Scientologists are prone to.

Uma Thurman and Ethan Hawke are spiritual, too, by
virtue of their worldly radiance. I was one of the first
people to know that Uma Thurman and Ethan Hawke
were having sex with each other. I saw them eating in a
restaurant together and deduced that they were having
sex with each other. Uma and Ethan: Two blond demigods
of blistering media sexuality. When they have sex, it must
be like twenty million people all having sex at the same
time, on one big floodlit stadium of a bed the size of Oahu.

A Massive Swelling

Ah, to be a famous person having sex with another famous person! The sheer mammoth narcissism of it all. Like slapping two movie screens together and making the films burn into each other under the projector's all-seeing white light. Like a sun swallowing another sun. I bet if you had a malignant tumor the size of a baseball on your neck and were under the bed when Ethan Hawke and Uma Thurman had sex, when they were finished, you would roll out and look in the mirror and the radiation would have sucked it down to the size of a small heart-shaped mole that somehow improved your appearance.

While in the restaurant, I was wearing an enormous white headdress from an African religious ritual I had attended earlier in the day. Ethan and Uma were intrigued. They poked around my table waving and smiling at me on their way out, as if my apparent religious eccentricity and their stardom were sort of *similar*, and my dedication to this unknown sect somehow qualified me for notice by them. "We know," their smiling and respectful faces seemed to say. Ethan didn't recognize me two nights later when I attended his theater benefit. I had swapped the white turban for a jeweled cat collar. I wasn't spiritually large with him anymore.

There is an inviolable bubble of invisible force around most stars that says, "Look if you have to, but under NO circumstances do you touch me in any way." This is something that is so thick and obvious that most people would reflexively throw up if faced with needing to infringe on this cosmic law, as it would just be dreadful beyond human reason to touch a star and suffer that "Please don't touch me" look. The most dreadful faux pas I've ever seen in a social setting involved Lou Reed. It was unbelievably ghastly, like a car accident involving a school bus and a drunk. I was taking a yoga class. There were two aging hipsters in the room with me, whom I didn't particularly notice at first, then realized were Laurie Anderson and Lou Reed. The yoga teacher was a big gregarious blonde, who had obviously been through some shit in her life and had overcome it with a big sense of positive identity, earned the hard way. "Does anybody in the class have any pain or injuries?" asked the teacher, who was known for her highly unorthodox flair for walking up to her pupils and eliciting horrible gritty ricochet sounds from their joints and vertebrae—which is something most teachers won't do, because of the inherent dangers of making a mistake and sending some poor klutz to the hospital. Bravely, Lou Reed, in his unmistakable Lou Reed cigarette-exhale drawl, told the teacher that he had a hip injury, obviously some form of premature bone-crumbling brought on by the total assassination of his body's calcium by his legendary lifestyle. The yoga teacher was doing a fine job of not-treating-the-stars-with-much-more-attention-than-the-other-students, randomly bouncing about the room filled with groaning secretaries forming fleshy triangles, and snapping misplaced bone and tissue masses back into their proper holes.

Then she got to Lou.

She seemed to be trying to pull his leg off, for a moment, or bend it sideways into the small of his back as if he were a collapsible bicycle. Then there was a sound like the skull of a cat being popped with a hammer, and we were all treated to the superhuman howl of Thoroughly Famous Icon Lou Reed in Pain. The class stopped breathing and we knew by the alarms in our stomachs that something terribly WRONG had happened, on the level of electrons sailing out of their orbits or atoms falling in half. The Rule had been violated. Lou's celebrity bubble had been punctured by our big blond yoga instructor, who was now backing away from him with her eyes darkening into hell-swirling sockets in her head, like Peter Lorre trying to crawl under a wall of garbage in *M*. She was giggling with a terrible, harrowing anguish, and yelping "Oh my God, oh my God, are you OK? I'm so sorry, oh my God!" giggling and giggling, awash in this unspeakable public nightmare. Air left the room as the Order of the Universe scrambled to right itself from the unholy catastrophe that had just impossibly played out in front of us. Out of compassion and loyalty, the rest of the yoga instructor's students and I tried to die in quiet motionlessness on the floor, in order to remove the witnesses to her terrible blow of fate. We could see all of her hard-won, positive self-image spurting out of her like hot red life from a punctured artery. The horrible square wheel of time in anguish dragged grittily forward and we were forced to pantomime white-faced normalcy through the rest of the class, accepting a mildly perturbed "I'm all right, I'm OK" from Lou and pretending that we had all recovered. What we really needed to do was band together en masse as a yoga class and start kicking Lou in the ribs—not hard, just as kind of a friendly hazing, so that the Terrible Thing didn't seem like such a big deal.

But it *was* a big deal. Never touch a celebrity. Never speak until you are spoken to. Don't stare, and NEVER touch.

∎

As a result of how out-of-control celebrity has become— i.e., how overloved celebrities are and how underloved the common man—a thin level of social insurgency has arisen. The finest hair salons, locker rooms, and backstage bullpens are all propaganda headquarters that generate a dismal layer of celebrity rumor so venal that it goes into the realm of public myth.

I am speaking, of course, of Richard Gere with a gerbil lodged in his rectum; David Bowie (or Rod Stewart) passing out on stage and being rushed to the hospital to have his stomach pumped and the doctors removing eight quarts of jism; Stevie Nicks having her roadie blow cocaine up her ass since her nose was caving in; a noted action star's famous instructions on how to give his dick-pump-implant a blowjob to a prostitute in his trailer ("Caress the balls, stroke the shaft. Caress the balls, stroke the shaft"). Stallone and Travolta fucking each other on the set of *Staying Alive* was another good one.

The latest and greatest foul rumor has Harvey Keitel, on the set of *Eyes Wide Shut*, getting canned from the project for surreptitiously ejaculating into Nicole Kidman's hair. True nor not, I loved what that story said about the sentiments of Keitel towards Kidman and her dwarfy power-tool husband.

■

The public craves these terrible stories. They humanize the star. By the same token, I have found that it is normal and satisfying to fantasize about weirdly abusing specific vile celebrities with tortures custom-designed to suit the persona of the distasteful star. Don't we all crave justice when a particularly cringe-worthy icon offends our refined sensibilities? We seek to balance the wrong inherent in them, via punishment. These fantasies are not dangerous unless they become feasible. Check your reflexive desire for easy revenge by retreating into elaborate, baroque fantasies that achieve absolute poetic justice! That way, any attempt to abuse the offending icon in too swift or simple a manner is boring and fruitless. You expose yourself to the danger of visiting the mall where they are doing a book signing and advancing towards the table swinging your heavily buckled belt, with your eyes red and mirrorized, absent with fury. I have concocted a few starter fantasies for you, Gentle Reader, in the hopes that their difficulty of execution inspires you to create similarly complex revenges, and thereby aid you in avoiding a disruptive prison sentence.

I feel the ultimate tempering of Broadway Antichrist Neil Simon would involve a *Clockwork Orange*–style chair-strapping and forced eyelid parting, before nonstop camcorder tapes of annual law-firm talent shows.

I had a fantasy for years about Frank Sinatra, who in his

advanced stages of entropy was as powerless and damaged as a moth-eaten taxidermized owl. I felt he needed to balance the jawbreaking, Mafia-tough-boy, bitch-slapping-playboy hubris of his sexy years by living out the rest of his weak and feeble days wearing a terry-cloth pantsuit in a Plexiglas box in the middle of Times Square, adjoined in a Habitrail fashion with a similar box containing former President Reagan, enjoying the irreverent jocularity of full-blown Alzheimer's. Periodically, the two should have been forced to wrestle by means of electrical stimuli.

I know that I am not alone in the opinion that all of Kathie Lee Gifford's orifices should be hemmed shut by Filipino immigrants for six dollars, or that Tony Danza somehow requires being sewn inside the body of an uncomfortable chimp costume for the remainder of his adult life.

The truth is, so many insufferable celebrities, because of their chronic hubris, will doubtlessly disgrace *themselves* in the span of their own public lives, all that is required for justice to be served like a boiled chihuahua on a silver tray is a bit of patience.

■

Celebrity torture fantasies are not something to be stifled or curtailed. Benignly accepting the shameful antics of these inappropriately glorified ego-Caligulas is the thing to worry about. When one STOPS having such fantasies and finds a way to live harmoniously with the visages of the offending figures, one is dead inside and needs to retire to the forest and run about naked killing snakes with a pointy stick in order to reignite the embers of one's being. Hollywood itself needs all the earthquakes, fires, and riots it can get. Anything that can shake that mess and its inhabitants into some kind of connection with the planet is long overdue and desperately needed. If God doesn't do it, there's always napalm.

CHAPTER 11

Hi-Diddly-Dee, an Actor's Life for Me: Brown Dwarfs and Hungry Ghosts

Brown Dwarf: A theoretical type of small, starlike object, with less mass than small stars and more mass than large planets. Scientists believe brown dwarfs form as stars do, from the gravitational contraction of interstellar gas. Brown dwarfs do not have enough mass to become true stars. Brown dwarfs radiate energy at a much lower temperature than stars do. . . .
ENCARTA 98 DESK ENCYCLOPEDIA

> What do you want to do?
> Art.
> So why do you go out and make
> An exhibition of yourself?
> THE FALL (MARK E. SMITH),
> *"Arms Control Poseur"*

*T*heater has been single-handedly responsible for generating some of the most flamingly intolerable personalities in the American lexicon: archetypes such as the Old Ham, the brassy, loudmouth booze hounds who feel compelled to belt out their musical favorites whenever they are less than fifty feet away from a Casiotone mini-synthesizer, despite the cringing of others; the Trouper, that psoriasis-covered old-timer who might crawl to the auditorium bleeding out of both eyes but who heroically coughs through yet another suburban production of *The Music Man* because of his deep, sinister, Freemason-like commitment to the idea that "the Show Must Go On"; the Hoofer, any tragic homosexual in tap shoes; and the Old Pros, leagues of intense, temperamental, middle-aged, childless women with a dependence on various painkillers who are only Really Living when, wearing a feather boa, they are wantonly parking their bronzer-streaked breasts over an untuned upright piano, causing themselves to weep over their own rendition of "Over the Rainbow" in their bimonthly gig at the local steakhouse (at home, they have hysterical, bourbon-powered crying fits and a lot of stuffed animals).

Lately there's been a whole new breed of aspiring unfortunate theater archetypes. A lot of comics, actors, and performance artists Up-'n'-Coming on "the Fringe" have taken an extreme aesthetic swerve and become grossly confessional; their acts are infused with the black electrical fire of gruesome personal details: bewilderingly complicated sexual handicaps and crushing failures of personality, shameful emotional wounds. The object seems to be to peel back every layer of self-preservation and privacy that their egos could attempt to shelter them with and Expose, wrenching themselves inside-out and training the klieg light of stage attention on their Darker Selves. It often works on some emotional fakir-like level as a weirdly interesting purging; sort of like watching a self-exorcism, or someone with railroad spikes through his cheek upchucking on his own genitals. More often than not you feel compelled, as an audience member, to exterminate the performer.

There is something truly paralyzing about a bad solo performance onstage. When you are in an audience, and the performer up on stage is lousy with joylessness and fuming with some illness that makes him/her stulti-fyingly ignorant of the mores of human entertainment, there is an odd stasis that sets in; you just sit there and take it, and some iron cloud of gravity cools your blood into a slowly metabolizing reptile anxiety, push-ing you further and deeper into the chair, rendering you mute and so motionless you can barely drink your cock-tail. It's a horrible yet strangely addictive sensation, one akin to the sealed-ears-underwater feeling one associates with wandering half-drunk around all-night drugstores staring at the bright packages with no comprehension of their texts. Bad comedy and bad performance art provide a kind of easy mental masochism for me; a dumb and mild pain, like chewing all the skin off my thumbs. It is pleasant, I suppose, because nothing will get your mind off of your own short-comings like seeing some shit-twirling baboon flailing away on some forgotten little stage like a house afire, compulsively absorbing your unfocused rage and annoyance.

■

There are a couple of types of people who should simply not ever be allowed onstage. These people invariably get onstage anyway.

One type generally found in the "edgier," "underground" performance scenes is the In-Your-Face Acid Casualty, the rambling, non-sequitur guy with the Day-Glo poster paint on his nipples, who, after barking out untranslatable material for several minutes, eventually takes his pants off and resorts to stuffing some object up his ass. This guy can be found outside after the show is over, laughing to his friends: "Man, did you see that? I totally pissed everybody off! They didn't know what the fuck I was doing! It was great!" This is the guy whose zenith of fame arrives when he does some ultramoronic guerrilla annoyance stunt like hurling himself onstage into Bob Dylan's knees at a public event, with some unintelligible slogan scrawled on his chest in his own feces.

Another type is epitomized by a girl I used to see at open mikes around town and referred to as Treya. Treya is the unwitting victim of too much overpositive input. She's a tall girl in a big pair of boots who stomps in and immediately starts engaging in conversations with the performer on stage. She's very boisterous, very young, with big eyes full of wonder and no safe personal boundaries. Treya is the kind of person who, when she is in a room, has such loud energy she demands excessive attention from everybody and is disturbingly impossible to ignore. Her background is something like upper-middle-class Nantucket nectar, but now she's a gone-all-gonzo–Lower East Side–bisexual-until-I-get-out-of-Tisch-School-for-the-Arts kind of gal, a slumming debutante in combat boots, bein' a real free-wheelin' Free Sprit. "All RIGHT!" she yucks it up, real loud. Treya is one of those annoying children who shame-lessly made adults listen while she sang the Oscar Mayer song. Her parents were undoubtedly psychotherapists who gave her too positive a self-image. Then, too many dykes told her she was beautiful. They probably all sat around in her dorm room, dying to get into her ugly corduroy pants, saying "Oh my God, Treya, you're so TALENTED! You REALLY should go on stage. No, I'm serious—you're so FUNNY!"

No amount of prejudice and trepidation can prepare you for her act. She gets out her guitar, whimsically painted with fluorescent swirls (Oh my GOD, Treya, you're such an ARTIST!), then starts singing long, long joke-songs in-spired by dumb esoteric events that only her closest stoned friends could possibly appreciate or understand.

You need to learn shame to be a performer. I know that's a very stifling, non–New Age thing to say, but it is true. If you are going to repeatedly get onstage and brazenly suck air in front of people, you might as well be caning them in the knees and robbing them. Performers must have some obligation to entertain. It is the price of attention.

■

It's always hard and awful to meet unsuccessful actors who desperately want to be household names. Some are so outrageously strung out on any glimmer of Hollywood attention that even if they have already achieved some comfortable modicum of success, they would still peel and eat a live Girl Scout to have more. I have flukishly accepted a couple of tiny film roles in my life, just for the hell of it, and been exposed to some truly dark thespian behavior. On one film shoot, I was sharing my trailer with an attractive, older TV-star lady, positively floral with kindness towards her fans whenever we'd pass them on the street. I thought she was majestic, a good and selfless Queen of Proletarian Culture. Then we got on camera together, and I realized the woman was professionally hell-bent on usurping the maximum amount of acceptable camera attention she could skillfully wring out of the situation, with a life-or-death seriousness that made my liver curl with fear. She stomped on my lines like they were on fire, and I got out of her way; I could see she was an aging and jealous goddess whose ultravain ambitions would stop short of nothing. I knew she would easily crush and hide my limp body under the nearest production truck if my elimination meant she could stand more fully in the shots. And she wasn't even the worst person on the shoot to contend with, not by a long stretch. Movie extras are the most pathetic, ass-sucking spaniels in the world. These people will do anything, anything, to be on camera. They will stand directly in front of you, jabbering their résumés and dry-humping your pedal-pushers while the camera is rolling until some PA screams at them to move back for the fiftieth time. Jesus, Extra Boy, I wanted to ask, can any kind of fame be worth the Australian shit-crawl you're doing to get it? Their appalling behavior is exemplary of the grabby, Me-for-godsake-ME!! attitude that made me run screaming away from the acting profession.

These types of actors are also the people who will go horribly crazy if somebody they know, or vaguely know, gets famous. They have to take to their beds, it's *that bad*, their lives are *over*, they are in Hell. God hates them. They sink into a self-loathing depression that lasts years, and it's all they can think about: "That *fucking bitch* is famous and I'm *not?!?* God loves *Hitler* more than he loves *ME!!!* I'm so fucking tired of *living* this life!!"

■

There is a creepy breed of theater actor who treats every handshake and introduction to a new person as an opportunity to plumb and weasel furiously for possible connections into the Business. At any dinner party full of theater people, there's always some ascotted, gladhanding thespian ponce who Dale Carnegies you with the saccharine criminal aura of someone vying to involve you in insurance-related mail fraud, with eyes all full of "earnestness" and "sincerity" and an arm-pumping handshake-with-name-repetition. He seems to be, in a car-salesmanly manner, the nicest guy you could ever hope to meet, but lingering directly behind him is the ghost of himself in the future, just after he has achieved the Fame, walking past you in sunglasses with a cell phone in a shiny black suit, stepping on your foot and barking a big indulgent guffaw as he shoves your face aside with his expensive elbow. Just as I was recently meeting one of these guys, his woman danced in, sparkling with nerves—another archetype in the nether spheres of the invisible superambitious: a lanky, hair-flipping preener in a tight leather skirt with a big red mouth and lots of giggling, flirty mannerisms like a soft-porn Karen Black chippy from the early seventies, suffering from a kind of unconscious, pre–Gloria Steinem retrosexual persona. We call these Tanktop in December girls; there is a breed of young hotties who are so infected by L.A. sex platitudes that even in the midst of an East Coast snowstorm they insist on peeling all fourteen layers of clothes off as soon as they get indoors so they can hang out in a halter top or a thin slip, because they just can't bear the thought of not being an erotic showpiece for twenty minutes, even in the winter over their poached eggs. Somebody important *might not see their unrestrained nipples* if they dressed warmly. This is a tragic career error they *will not be making.*

The thespian's girlfriend shucked off her snakeskin leather jacket and minced pony-style to the table in a spaghetti-string camisole, sleet roaring outside the window like a frozen tidal wave.

"I'm a model, and an actress, and a playwright, and a

sculptress," she said when asked. Translation—always this translation, never not this translation—stripper.

They were breaking into "the Business" with incredible cartoon naïveté; you could just see them six months beforehand, arriving with cardboard suitcases in Times Square from some gray industrial cheese-processing town in the Midwest and looking up at the glittering lights and beating their chests and saying, "I'm gonna MAKE it! I'm gonna be a STAR on BROADWAY! Because I'm a WINNER!" There was something truly sweet about them and their big, frail dreams, though, that almost made me feel cruel as I jotted down notes about them on the host's napkins at the dinner table. They had found each other and were parts of the same socket set; they were trying to be good people—they were just a bit tarnished by simplicity and the lite sleaze that is the unmistakable flavor of Hollywood Lust.

The Thespian proudly informed me that he had been working as an intern for a prominent theater group—a job I knew well. I had many friends who had gone through that sorry résumé booster—essentially, it consisted of fetching coffee and stuffing envelopes for the vainglorious privilege of being within twenty feet of the Great Clique for six months, all for free.

"That's tough work," I said in genuine sympathy. Nobody gives a rat's ass about interns.

"Oh, NOOOO. It was really a wonderful EXPERIENCE. I met a lot of people in the INDUSTRY *blah, blah* POSITIVE ENERGY *blather, dribble.*"

166

I shook my head for him. There's nothing you can do for that type, who are militantly hell-bent on acting superior to you by pretending to love eating shit, New Age–style. These are the people for whom no compromise is too intense for the sake of what might be future applause. Many of these people become very famous, *All About Eve*–style; they get the doors of some Inner Sanctum to open a crack for them through grotesque fawning toadyness, then beat their way inside and overpromote themselves with the rude adamancy of Visigoths. The ones who don't become famous themselves generally end up in some proximity to famous people, and fall into some aspect of managing their careers, and the bitterness turns them very, very evil.

The saddest thing of all is the fact that the "Broadway" these actors so crave—i.e., a live, tough and discriminating audience falling giddily in love with them and recognizing their mighty talents as the pinnacle of excellence—is a Broadway that doesn't really exist. Broadway is just as deplorably fucked and lame as all the other entertainment institutions that have been artistically ramrodded up the keister by a corporate agenda.

Here in an age where all of our images must be premasticated by a prior decade and regurgitated from the mouths of bankers, there is little hope that any theater project that is actually "new" or "cutting edge" or "shocking" will ever make it out of the underground garage. Even the "shocking" images of twenty years ago are too rough for the Broadway audience of today. Now that all of our artistic media are financially dominated by the saccharine and banal, this is the only material that receives serious promotion. There will always be a place for the more challenging themes, but these are ghettoized into angry-at-the-world, underfinanced areas that nobody visits very often because they're such a "downer."

•

In 1995, I realized that everything I ever thought Broadway represented—i.e., the topmost artistic achievements of the theater—was ball-sucking malarkey after seeing the Broadway version of The Who's *Tommy*, which made me feel as if all of the sex and character had been scoured from my person with an abrasive white cleanser. *Tommy* was once a Hold Your Freak Flag High manifesto that had some marvelously foul imagery, particularly in its movie treatment by Ken Russell: who can forget Ann-Margret writhing orgiastically with her legs knotted around a satin tube pillow, with baked beans being vomited over her from the screen of a big TV? Or the screaming hair and thighs of a death-voltage Tina Turner? Or the plaintive religious vacancy in the eyes of Roger Daltrey?

"Rock" is supposed to be an institution dedicated to the destruction of the values that castrated this musical: i.e., pandering to the paralyzing ideals of weepy Christian hausfraus and the cash money ideologies that implement ruthless mainstream sanitizing. Watching this glossy corpse of what was once a vervy piece of unimpeded Rock was like trying to eat and digest a bowl of plastic daisies; all original *Tommy*-ness had been blanched and whipped into marshmallow toothpaste and shameless golden showers of sugar water.

What I really wanted was to be gripped by the ankles and sucked down a monstrous wet throat full of fanged nudes and opium cherry bombs and hoarse psychedelic voice-torture, as befitting the function of "rock." Instead, the Broadway Tommy ponced about pirouetting and blathering out candied vibrato in an eighth-grade Artful Dodger accent, in front of stage images no more emotionally challenging than the big lunchroom number of *Grease* or Little Orphan Annie stomping her widdle foots.

Perhaps the whole idea of "rock" on Broadway is simply a tremendous and irreconcilable misstep, but it is becoming increasingly apparent that absolutely anything can be utterly ruined by being made into a new Broadway show, including old Broadway shows. When the horrifying Broadway retread of *Annie Get Your Gun* premiered in 1999, there were many subsequent articles bemoaning its success despite the thrashings of every smart critic in New York. The show rolled on undeterred, fueled by millions in advance ticket sales to tourists, and the beatings registered nary a welt on its chuckity-chuckling hide. Nobody listens to the critics: the reign of Frank Rich is over, and critics no longer have any kind of real power to sculpt the taste of the masses anymore, because everybody stopped worrying about being tasteless when they stopped reading papers in favor of staring walleyed at Roger Ebert's thumb. Case in point: *Angels in America* by Tony Kushner, easily the best piece written for the theater in the last twenty-five years, survived only a year or two on Broadway even after winning every conceivable award, whereas there was an enormous and indestructible shrine erected to the 6,978,072nd performance of *Cats* at the Winter Garden, which boasted the ominous marquee NOW AND FOREVER, as if the show wielded some kind of unquestionable force in the universe, like hydrogen or Satan—and it almost DID.

Maybe if Tony Kushner had really wanted people to listen to his ideas about AIDS, he should have put Roy Cohn in a bunny suit and had him sing (a game plan which ended up being the driving force behind the success of the musical *Rent,* a play that is, for all intents and purposes, *Cats* with AIDS). The high-ticket-buying entertainment audience of today is not interested in any kind of emotionally difficult, wailing catharsis, which is the religious intention of theater dating back to its origins. Those who handle the big money tend to act as if they feel that catharsis is better managed through interpretive ice-skating or a song sung by Winnie-the-Pooh. I feel that there are few things more offensive than empty, overhyped schlock that is supposed to move and thrill an audience while being completely drained of its real intellectual and/or emotional content. The only thing possibly more offensive is the fact that the audience itself is now so empty and well trained and schlock-addicted that it is indeed moved by these fatty theatrical dry humps, and keeps coming back, Now and Forever.

As long as there are audiences that love and attend

these overproduced Muppet sing-alongs that are being pimped to the public as the Cream of Theater, there will be inflatable dancing boys and girls with round red mouths who believe they will only be truly happy when all that top-audience sucker-love is aimed at them. I knew what would happen to my couple at the dinner party. The Thespian would end up a phone lackey in some agent's office, sizzling with fiberoptic proximity to big stars like John Turturro or Mariel Hemingway every time he said "Just a minute, I'll get him," and social-drinking until all the veins in his nose exploded into red trees. The stripper would always be a stripper, despite aspirations to the contrary. Maybe she could get chewed to death by robot dogs while lathering her breasts in some big-screen sci-fi horror travesty, but she would never really be able to get away from the Big Money of the Naked Night enough to retire her vinyl thong and wake up early enough to throw on a baseball hat and audition at ten A.M. for some nonpaying legit theatrical project. Some big mook would marry her someday, and she'd have a little dog and a big television.

It all reminded me of the hapless fame-seeking of Dorothy Stratten in *Star 80:* her dumb trust in the benevolence of the Lucky Star, which turns out to be a shiny piece of cardboard with a bug light in front of it, pointing the way to the Tijuana donkey show. There's NOOOOO Business Like SHOOOOOOOOOW Business Like NOOOOOOOOOO Business I KNOOOOOOW. Find a better hobby, I want to say to all the unfortunate kids who crave the Life of the Stage to the point of total self-mortification. Get married and move to Jacksonville, Florida. Teach drama and tumbling to the young. Launder thy souls in things humble and humane; perhaps then you will be Whole.

CHAPTER 12

You Will Now Watch the Hollywood Awards Ceremony

*R*un! Set bonfires about the Great Temple! Throw down thy finest fattened goats and honor the marble halls with their warm blue entrails and spouts of pulsing arterial blood! Quickly, wretch! Squeeze a hen, polish the largest fruits; consecrate the bronze and tusklike member of a nearby satyr with the hymen of your youngest wailing daughter! Understand ye not?!! The Movie Gods have demanded another fest in honor of their golden heroes!!! Dress the slaves in ocelot skins and let them club one another to death in mock jazz-dance battle! Sacrifice and sing with mouth afroth! Like all of the other filthy, illiterate villagers, I am faint and vomiting from the euphoric strain.

Every year at Oscar time it's the same fever-faced bacchanal: the world stops; wars apparently roll up and vanish, whole oceans rot, whole countries, races, and species are bulldozed into mulch and forgotten while the entire dog-eyed population of mankind whimpers and presses their noses against the palace window at the unregenerate, obscenely grandiose, self-congratulatory orgies of the culturally moribund entertainment world, the various award shows. Our self-loathing society loves to decide that a certain elect group of people are Superuntouchable, Caesaresque Divine Royalty that get to have the most material possessions and unceasing, sycophantic attention and love. And what compels us, the Great Unwashed, to actually scramble over one another to *watch* awards shows where the same fifty-two reshuffled famous people get to lick each other and pat each other's silky buttocks and squeak out corporate Valentines for the same mind-blowingly mediocre accomplishments, year after year? It's SHOW BIZ!!! We love and hate it desperately and masochistically, the same way that peasants despised and idolized the drunk aristocrats who terrorized their streets and used their heads as impromptu polo balls on medieval Saturday nights.

Here is a guide to everything needed for a complete evening of celebrity glorification, guaranteed to hypnotize and commercially pimp-slap the weak-minded and terminally devoid of fabulousness—i.e., everyone who isn't famous.

■

To have a big awards ceremony, first you must hire a hugely successful Leading Name Brand of comic emcee: for the big events, Billy Crystal or Whoopi Goldberg; for smaller events, someone "edgy" (but not Chris Rock—he's too edgy).

Billy Crystal is so utterly relaxed and pleasant in front of everybody in the world that it doesn't matter what he says, he's just comforting to watch. Let Whoopi say "Shit!" occasionally, because she's black, after all. It will make the whole event seem almost warmly human for a minute or two.

Robin Williams can't host, because he has to be in the audience; usually because he's nominated for something—some film where he plays the kindly dying-children's doctor gifted with unusual pep and compassion, who pulls balloon animals out of his own ass.

You could get Rosie O'Donnell, but, well, I think her enthusiasms have been flogged to death by overuse. She's been enthusiastic about everything from dried food products to infant appliances to KMart. She has become the nicest, most pedantic woman in America. But hey! She's perfect for *Sesame Street* count-a-thons or the Special Olympics with that big daytime-TV, overenunciating-for-the-hearing-impaired-and-high-school-dropouts mouth on her, God love that woman. She's got pep, and she's also got a certain degree of that other main celebrity love requirement: ubiquity!

■

When all of the celebs are milling around outside of the auditorium showing their shoes to the photographers, it is a necessary, equalizing experience for the proles at home if some celeb wears an ugly dress. Everybody needs to see a star look bad. We all love to make fun of the generally dowdy Diane Keaton, who always shows up wearing some senior-citizen-drunk-at-the-Off-Track-Betting-parlor look; one year she appeared to be wearing a rhinestone whiplash brace, and it was important to those of us watching the event on TV from unclean apartments. Cher once wore a headdress that made her look like an S&M century cactus. How about that year when Demi Moore showed up in that black bustier ensemble that made her look like a bicycle-racing hooker from the Old West? Susan Sarandon always looks like she stapled her own dress together out of recycled cabbages and hemp. The Redgrave sisters and Barbra Streisand were always good for terminally dated grooming, from weatherproofed Chinese bob-bouffants to Egyptian beanhead 'fros and guard-rail-sized liquid eyeliner.

At the '99 Oscars I loved wondering what the fuck those makeup artists were thinking with that popular Damp Actress look. Was that glittering, unpowdered facial effect supposed to simulate a youthful dewy fecundity? Their foreheads were runny. It looked like the malaria sweats from where I was sitting, and no white woman was immune.

A Massive Swelling

•

Next, the audience needs to see the bow-tied head of a Truly Affable Guy, and that guy is Tom Hanks. The Affable Guy has become indispensable.

Robin Williams was AG #1; then it was Hanks, and it's been Hanks for quite a while—since 1988, when he was nominated for Best Actor in (of all things) *Big*. Lately, Tom Hanks has gotten kind of bizarre, though. It started in 1993, when he gave his over-the-top, tearful New Age humanitarian acceptance speech for *Philadelphia*, during which he mentioned "our creator" and "America" a few too many times. In '99 he was wearing a thickness of unsightly hair on both cheeks and looked Serious and Disturbed, with the flat-nail-head eyes of someone who has suddenly learned to fear Jesus while on a terrifying megahit of pharmaceutical-grade acid. Hanks might be turning into a gooned-out patriot, or a Rasputin-like recluse à la Matthew Broderick, who is living proof that the "nice guy" role can make someone just as internally cockeyed as a kidney-damaged child star. Perhaps Tom has embraced a backwoods snake-handling cult. The World War II films got him all spooky; he started looking like he wanted to salute astronauts or wade bravely through billowing flags.

OK, forget Tom Hanks. How about Will Smith?! There's no stopping the affability of that guy! He's the Tom Hanks of Rap! He's the Affable Party Dude of the new millennium!! Every summer box-office weekend is a

Will Smith Weekend! Cut to reaction shot of his comely brown wife. I feel "jiggy" all over!

.

Somebody really important—i.e., the most talked-about, famous person of the whole year—needs to be obviously missing. This makes all of the remaining celebrities look better, and poses a lot of interesting questions for the dog people at home.

At the *Titanic* Oscars, all one could really ask themselves was "Where was El DiCaprio?" Was he off learning to become a Scientologist in order to cure himself of tabloid homosexuality? Was he deflowering non-English-speaking supermodels? ("Yes, I have LOVE for you. *Amour . . . amore . . .* Whatever. Where are the snaps on this thing?") Cowering with Michael Jackson in the petting zoo? Grinding up a sandwich bag of Peruvian Flake in the strobe-lit VIP womb of the Viper Lounge and jabbering about real estate? Crying on the couch with a team of Jungian therapists who massaged his hands and read him mythology and Joseph Campbell? ("Yes, Leo—*fame hurts*. Look what it did to Perseus. Do you really think you should take another Xanax?") Where was the shiny boy who was in the terrifying jockey position of being the Ubiquitous Person of the Moment Who Would Be Loved into Pulpy Matter by Blindly Devouring Fans? At the time, he had something like four photo albums of himself on the *New York Times* Best-Seller List, his little childish jawline fixed on "manly" setting, his eyes staring earnestly off into the middle distance; but at the Oscars, Leo was nowhere to be found. It was like *Sesame Street on Ice* with no Big Bird. The Great Robot Hollywood is hardwired to always leave its audience *wanting*.

■

Next, villains are introduced, for drama: the goddamned BRITS. The classically trained British actors in the audience make all our American actors look like heartfelt, impoverished bumpkins; like a Jamaican bobsled team at the Nazi Olympics. The Brits are basically a lot more talented and glamorous than we are, so we have to set them up and make them look as if they might win something, in order that our plucky, down-home American heroes might beat them, as if to say: We American actors may be untrained and illiterate, but we can beat you imperialist snobs with homegrown courage and the patchwork spirit of the frontier! Virtuoso Emily Watson with her big sad eyes and frowny little mouth can show up every year if she wants to, but she won't get an ounce of love from Hollywood until she guest-drowns on *Baywatch*. When the "Aw, shucks!" American wins and can't believe it, cut to Geoffrey Rush glowering with his terrible skin condition.

■

Now it's time for the coveted "Verge of Death" Award. Who's that super-old guy again? James Coburn? Mel Brooks? Let him ramble a bit with the trophy clutched in his painful-looking arthritic fists. Cut to his nineteen-year-old wife with the outrageous EE-cup techno-hooties.

Maybe give him a chance to prove he isn't quite dead yet, like when Jack Palance proclaimed "Billy Crystal? I crap bigger than him," and started doing one-armed pushups next to the podium. When Bette Davis or any other old Hollywood barnacle starts babbling on and on and on because they're so old and overindulged they think they are immune to television rules, the orchestra suddenly kicks in and slowly gets louder and louder until they can't babble any more belligerent-old-person tangent-patois. Then tall women in black dresses drag them hobbling off the stage.

∎

Next, a really lame technical yawner award like Best Sound Editing needs to go to the surprisingly good movie of the year, the inexpensive, soulful, unexpected delight, which usually gets all the media nonattention of a nine-year-old kid's first efforts on the camcorder, or a Bombay softcore.

∎

Around this point, the camera needs to start hovering around the patient, ironed head of Celine Dion, nominated for Best Eye-Bleeding Vocal in a Movie, looking like she's waiting to win the best of breed in the Westchester Anorexia Cup. The sighting of Celine triggers the beginning of the aesthetically harmful halftime-entertainment quotient.

First, switch on that Turbo Karaoke Emotion, and get ready to tear up and start coughing out money, 'cause it's time for the social-consciousness number, the one about AIDS, which I like to call the "We Gawn Sing Dat Big Disease Away, Lawdy Lawdy" song.

I guess that ever since "We Are the World" there is a general idea that if you pack as many hollering people onto a "good cause" album as possible, you are somehow creating an Emotional Experience (read: $$$$$$$$). However, it ain't a big hit unless it has a big fat gospel choir descending out of the rafters in white robes and a special verse sung by Bono Vox of U2. Bono, Charity Whore, is always willing to wave his arms in the air for AIDS sentimentalism, whilst all the churchified Africans try to outsoul each other, and erupt into unrestrained combat-wailing. From hospital beds across America, sick people must be thinking, "Damn, that was powerful. I wish I had AIDS, instead of one of the hundreds of other uncool diseases killing people every year!" Hollywood loves that AIDS.

Next, why have a truly interesting, top-o'-the-cultural-heap dance company like the Dance Theatre of Harlem or Pina Bausch or Mark Morris perform, when you can have a perplexing *Flashdance*-esque "interpretive" mega-embarrassment dance-boner brazenly hack-sawed out by ex-*Fame* Gorgon-choreographer Debbie Allen? How about a pulsating, floor-denting flamenco dance by a sweaty, shirtless Spaniard in sausage-tight bootlegged dance-pants, set to a totally incongruous swoopy film-orchestra number? It'll be great! Then she'll humiliate poor Savion Glover by making him try to tap out more beatless movie-violin mush, with the entire audience clutching each other's elbows in fright. It's always good to have some mind-blowingly bad art that everybody has to shudder through, in order to make the big lip-synchings that happen later appear more dynamic.

Or even better than Debbie Allen: a little visit by Mike Flatley's *Lord of the Dance*, Jesus save our poor imperiled souls! Flatley! The hopping, bucking satyr in the rubber bolero jacket, cock package, and leather headband! Seeing him at an awards ceremony is sort of like peeking into Oscar's top drawer and seeing a two-foot black strap-on dildo on top of a bunch of Zamfir CDs.

■

All this excitement warms us up for the coup de grâce, which is generally Madonna. Celine Dion may be a worthless establishment whore, a simpering, white-cake Karen Carpenter stroking the most banal nerve denominator in the music industry, but she still sounds a lot better than Madonna.

Madonna has probably indirectly or directly influenced my life more than any other celebrity; I've always appreciated the thingness of Madonna. But Madonna has always looked naked to me at the Oscars, because at the Oscars there's usually six or seven truly talented people in the audience, and she's performing in front of them, and they can see exactly what she is, and she knows it, and she's always shivering with fear and bracing herself with that steely "You Must Love Me" breed of tenacity she's always had. She did it with some forgettable *Dick*

Tracy number a few years back, and after *Evita* she felt compelled to cry real tears singing the Andrew Lloyd Webber snore lullaby because she knew she couldn't actually sing it, and decided to balance out her lack of pipes with some "acting" that the folks could appreciate. "My, she can cry on cue, just like an Actress," we were meant to say, not noticing her weak, tremulous, dumb-musical-theater voice. It was like watching your cousin in a high-school talent show sing some bad slow song real sincerely with too much vibrato, wherein the guilelessness of it hurts because she isn't very good and it's cringe-worthy. It always becomes blindingly clear, whenever she has done this, that Madonna isn't a singer, and should go with that thing she does do, which I guess is be personally interesting and indomitably superfamous, like Courtney Love, who now has the advantage over Madonna of being able to play herself on film.

■

After thirty-five minutes of commercials, we head straight for Jack Nicholson.

When Jack Nicholson won the Best Actor Oscar in '98, I remember thinking, Jesus, could that desiccated old vampire really have churned out a Nicholson performance so starkly different from all the other Nicholson performances that he merited a whole new trophy?

But Nicholson is a permanent fixture at the Oscars; he's always there, looking like they keep him in a big tank of grain alcohol all year long, then lift him out by crane for the Oscars and wring him out, ironing the tuxedo directly on his fearful body, so he can be that scary wedge-toothed Nicholson thing he is, lurking blackly and Nicholsonesquely in the aisle seat, forever.

I'm convinced that Jack Nicholson and Warren Beatty have the same disease. It's an obscure ailment that you can see in several of today's Hollywood gentlemen. Beatty has always been famous for being great-looking, with his big body and wavy hair, and heterosexual. This, combined with the fact that he was famous in the seventies, has made him one of the most consistently oversexed crea- tures in the world, right up there with Wilt Chamberlain and Magic Johnson's magic johnson. Getting too much snatch over too many years has made Warren, as well as Jack Nicholson and a host of other men famous for playing versions of themselves, somewhat frightful and insane; Warren Beatty and Jack Nicholson are Pussy Sick. Pussy Sickness seems to embalm all of its sufferers in such a way that they age slowly and evilly into looking like their heads are sculpted out of raw beef, and they *never go away*.

I imagine Warren Beatty's pre-marriage sex life as a little something like this: Warren, in darkened limousine, is stalking down Rodeo Drive or Sunset Boulevard, with a small list on a clipboard of the fretfully specific types of woman he hasn't yet had sex with: a twenty-four-year-old Iranian virgin on her last field trip before returning to the Middle East to her arranged marriage. A redheaded French stewardess with an overbite. A lisping nursery-school teacher with an alluring facial scar.

WARREN: Excuse me, miss?

A Massive Swelling

Miss: Oh my God, Warren BEATTY!

Warren: Do you have any little red boots?

Miss: Um . . . what??

Warren: Boots. Red. Ankle-length. Have you got any?

Miss: Well . . . no, I . . .

Warren: Do you know where we could get some?

Woman nervously enters limo. Two hours later she is shoved out of limo, drunk, tousled, little red boots on, at a nearby 7-Eleven, with a shiny quarter so she can use the pay phone. Another type is banished from the checklist with an aggressive scribbling of black Mont Blanc fountain pen. Warren wads up his ruined necktie, pulling another out of a spare champagne bucket. He and driver squeal out of the parking lot, back into the bloodline of populated streets.

Pussy-Sick men get a wobbly look in their eyes, a kind of overpermissiveness with themselves that after fifty just starts to look like a kind of omnipresent leer: the toxic sheen of bending too many kneesock'd girls-young-enough-to-be-their-daughters over benches in secluded sculpture gardens.

Bill Cosby is a sufferer of Pussy Sickness, as was Uncle Milty. Kevin Costner has it. I thought Costner would be reduced to doing Chuck Wagon commercials by now: you know, being a macho, expressionless spokesman for some kind of Marlboro-Mannish, hickory-dickory-dunce honky-cowhick egomaniac peckerwood crap, heee-yuk. But Costner's still here, muttering around in the background, not listening to the acceptance speeches, hitting on the tall boobie girls who escort the stars on and off the stage.

Woody Allen has a whole different type of porno affliction. Woody, needy, concave, shriveled little man that he is, always needs to be portrayed in his own films as the Dynamic Priapic Masterpiece for Whom All Young Women Throw Their Skirts Over Their Heads. "God, you were just amazing!" the woman thirty-six years his junior whimpers and pants while they lie in the dark. "No, really, I've never had such incredible sex, it was really, really moving." There needs to be a sex scene between Woody and Barbra Streisand, in order to do karmic justice to them both.

Warren Beatty has the additional affliction of being attracted to politics, and politics has never been a pretty thing for an actor to pursue. We can all laugh now, watching old footage of that Indian babe accepting the award for Brando. "What a kook he was," we can say to ourselves, "trying to get all political with those weird brown people! He must have just been drunk that day, or too darn fat!" There's a moment in every awards ceremony where a politically uncomfortable twinge goes through the audience as they all simultaneously think: Oh, shit . . . Susan Sarandon is about to say something vegetarian. Uh-oh, Spike Lee is here, representing his mean little films that so hate Whitey. Vanessa Redgrave is yowling about the Palestinians again.

■

It's around this time that an award goes to some chilling, expensive little documentary about the Holocaust, Hollywood's favorite genocide.

A Massive Swelling

The Academy gets tired and cranky viewing the black plight, or other plights that they are not a part of and therefore do not understand. Nobody seriously thought they'd rally behind the Branch Davidians and give the documentary Oscar to *Waco: Rules of Engagement,* perhaps the most chilling, revealing documentary about our present police-state mentality, or *The Farm,* a heavyhearted window into our prison system. Why recognize a new, present villain like the ATF, or a genocide-in-progress like the plight of the young black male, when you can trot those photogenic Nazis out, year after year?

When Spielberg won the Oscar for Best Director in '99, the sky above the stage opened and a mystical sun came streaming through a hole in the jellyfish-like dome: "Look," my friend screamed, already embarrassed for what he was about to say, "God has come to collect his favorite Jew!" Now look, those Sons and Daughters of Israel deserve a lot of credit, OK, OK, I'm not trying to say "The Holocaust is over, let's get on with life" or anything, but Jesus, atrocious violations of human rights happen every single day. You'd think impending murders would have some clout over ones committed fifty years ago, but noooooooooooo, not to the guys who cut the checks in the Emerald City.

Hoop Dreams, one of the best documentaries ever made, wasn't even nominated in 1994. Remember *Amistad?* I had a feeling it would be totally ignored; all those Calvin Kleiny fashion shots of heartbreakingly muscular black athletes, writhing for survival in a cruel and ignorant early America. "You watch," I said, when *X* came out. "This year won't be one of what the Academy must refer to as their Noble Cripple & Spade years. They'll trot Denzel onstage to present Best Sound Effects Editing in a Foreign Short Film, and that'll be all she wrote." Yup. And that's egg-zacktly what happened. Why honor any more black people? asketh the Academy. We have Whoopi!

∎

The Oscars also can't quite deal with Latin people.

For some reason, whenever a man or woman of Latin origin is accepted by the Hollywood industry giants, they have to be either hundreds of frenetic degrees wigglier or traumatically more oversexed than any American person, or both.

First they trot out Sophia Loren, wearing a demure breast maturity veil, following a photomontage of her breasts in better days.

Then they pan over to Antonio Banderas, who began his career looking like an elegant Spanish architect, then came to America, married collagen accident Melanie Griffith, and became an absurdly chest-shaved, pumped and basted romance-novel panty dampener with oily Prince Valiant hair and an open pirate blouse, pouting and ready to rip the strings off his leather pants for aggressive lovemaking.

In '99 we had Roberto Benigni, Italian, sproinging around like a big naked rabbit shouting how he wanted to "make love with you all," reflecting both outrageous wiggliness and oversexedness.

Jennifer Lopez, one of Hollywood's favorite hood ornaments, while in possession of a peeling rack, always comes off like she needs more vocal training from her acting coach so she doesn't sound so much like she grew up deep in the barrio carving "Chicas Locas" into her thigh with a Bic pen. She seems hyperconscious of this; she is kind of begging for somebody like Celine Dion's unsmiling dungeonmaster to Henry Higgins her into a real Lady. J. Lopez needs to go to charm school to learn how to be charming, but in Hollyworld, being Puerto Rican and having a salacious buttocqueria is enough. They always let her represent the tits and ass of Puerto Rico, so that whenever a person of Latin origin takes the stage, the camera can cut to her for a racked-out-Latina reaction shot.

■

When it comes to sentimental porn, the Academy has made it perfectly clear that Retards are the order of the day. Whenever an actor takes on the jibbers and tics of a palsied or otherwise "challenged" character, the Academy has fallen all over itself to shower the actor with praise. This has been true ever since *The Miracle Worker.* Anybody portraying somebody with the boot print of a clumsy god pressed into his or her forehead—any dramatic role with waggling palsied wrist action or a dragging clubfoot and a tongue like a tennis ball—will take home a naked gold man on Oscar Night. These unsubtle gimmicks have beaten out more delicate emotional characterizations so systematically over history that every fall we are now besieged by more Triumphs of the Lame.

The Academy has never figured out that these spasms and tics are way easier than simply delivering an emotionally complicated line.

∎

Many stars are obviously fucked-up on something.

You can't really tell who might be humming with stimulants because they could just be aggressively facelifted into a constant look of surprise, like Cher. George Lucas always seems moodily drunk, and looks like an enormous pink brain coral. De Niro must have been squiffy when he got that haircut that made him look like a fat, mean pineapple.

∎

If it seems like you're seeing the same people at your awards ceremony year in and year out, well, you are. I was confused about it for a while, but then the truth hit me like a sack of fan mail: America, as a whole, can only be truly aware of a limited number of personalities outside of their own lives. The shuffling deck of celebrity has about fifty-two heads, and we are served "hands" of about seven or less at a time, and these appear on every book and magazine cover in the world for a little while, and then they go back to the bottom of the deck again, only to resurface several months later. This is the course of things. Those whom we are seeing now, we will continue to see in heavy rotation for the next two or three years, like ubiquitous pop songs. Those who were models become actresses, those who were actors become directors; but the face cards are all the same, and everybody in that deck is only there because they are somehow masturbation fodder to big cross sections of ignorant, bacon-eating, maladjusted rural folk, who are dazzled by the whole spectacle like infants before jangling house keys, and for some reason, Cher is the Joker, and no matter how many cards get bumped or rotated, Cher is always there, getting played out again and again.

■

Right before the big prizes come up, it's time to trot out the forgettable Irving J. Something-or-Other award to some forgettable guy who did a lot of great things in the past. The old guy will say something profound and pointed to the new breed of ruthless success-seekers, such as something to the effect that film has forgotten how to celebrate the Joy of Living, or that filmmakers should pay more attention to a good story than the big money. "Hmmm," all the Big Players in the audience say, chin in hand, nodding, as if to say, "Too true," when inside they are all saying, "Ha ha ha ha ha, oh ha ha ha ha." When this righteous old crabapple is out of the way, everyone will have urinated and had a sandwich.

■

The success of the movie *Titanic* proved once and for all that the Oscars are the Grammies of film, and that nothing in the entertainment industry matters except huge sweaty dogpiles of banally earned cash. Ironically, *Titanic* also provided some of the most deplorable winners and losers the Oscars had ever seen.

You knew that Kate Winslet felt severely robbed when the Best Actress Oscar went to Helen Hunt. You could tell by the way the black foam started pouring out of her mouth. You knew Kate had her entire night planned around flashbulb handshakes and gracious Lovegetting. La Winslet's greasy curls looked more and more Medusa-like throughout the evening; you could tell that she needed the Oscar for sick personal reasons. She was going to go back to the hotel, get shitfaced, and eat twenty-four Ho-Hos, sobbing and spitting and throwing ashtrays out the window. FUCK the Oscars! FUCK them!

Buh-hoo-hoooo-hoooo-hooo-hooo. Sniff. Buh-hoo-hoo-hoo. All that crucial nationwide masturbation was happening over DiCaprio, and nobody was hanging posters of her.

James Cameron's grotesquely self-aggrandizing speeches for his *Titanic* Oscars proved once and for all that he's a totally loathable Costnerian dullard and an ego-bloated dunce. "I'm King of the World!" he screamed, like an alpha-baboon on a hill of his own shit, replacing "I'd like to thank all the little people" as the most fatuous Oscar-winning speech of all time.

•

Then the big Best Actress Award goes to: the prettiest and youngest American actress who had her face on the most magazine covers. Why? She's gonna make Hollywood and any brand of clothing or makeup she wears all the babysitting money earned in the entire nation this year.

■

There must have been a time when the Oscar winners reflected the votes of the outside world too, and were not just the vanity parade of some elite group of fame-community power faces and their superagents. Now Hollywood is an organism totally out of control, governed only by the weird preferential swells of box-office economics and strange inner-political strangleholds à la Harvey Weinstein. Remember, the great work of art always has to lose to the heartwarming money pile: *Network*, one of the ten best movies ever made, lost to *Rocky*, which went on to birth *Rocky*s 2, 3, 4, and 5, and the inescapable reign of stumpy cockmonger Stallone for the next two decades. *Apocalypse Now*, one of the grand artistic triumphs of American cinema, lost to—get this—*Kramer vs. Kramer*. In 1965, Herb Gardner's *A Thousand Clowns*—perhaps the only movie I have ever considered to be "heartwarming"—lost to the cocksucking *Sound of Music*. To believe that a good movie won a Best Picture Oscar because it was a good movie and not because it had a hugely aggressive, sharklike, zillion-dollar campaign is to clap your hands because you believe in pretty little faeries. A closer glimpse at Hollywood's inner workings reveals that the only real faeries are the hairy little perverts in the tulle ballgowns who will pay big money to have their crotches professionally stepped on with tall black shoes. The low-brow sponsorship usually sums it all up in a flash: The Oscars, brought to you by Kentucky Fried Chicken, Camaro, and JCPenney. Yep.

■

Hoo! Now it's time for the fabulous "After" parties!

A journalist girlfriend of mine was covering a party that voting New York Members of the Academy attended at famous Elaine's. "How were they?" I asked, wondering what the Academy people looked like.

"Prunes. Awful. Sucked dry," she said.

"Any stars?"

"Old, old Chita Rivera, Sylvia Miles, and Tina Louise—Ginger from *Gilligan's Island*."

"Octogenarian Trim."

"Exactly. Old slags who couldn't get invited to the real one."

I pictured some hairy old white vulture gawking at the rivulets of puckering skin down the neckline of Tina Louise, trying to get her fucked-up on Frangelico. Ow.

■

Everyone in the world knows that there is only one real party: the one thrown by Harvey Weinstein or Puff Daddy or *Vanity Fair* or Tina Brown, which is all basically the same party—the AAAA+ list, where everyone victoriously famous will ecstatically meet everyone else who is victoriously famous, and breakfast steam trays will roll out at six A.M. and the lucky will still be going strong with their little statuettes, on the vivid, life-amplifying power of Stardom. Everyone else may as well be clawing a wet tunnel under the post office in order to hang out with the voles. I know that's what I'll be doing next year.

CHAPTER 13

The Two-Headed Calf

Due to some rather dubious personal connections, I was invited, a few years ago, to attend the birthday party of Kato Kaelin, the lawnmowing, purportedly narcotics-friendly suckboy who perched impishly on the corpse of O. J. Simpson's reputation, at the height of The Trial. I thought it would be an unforgettable sociological learning experience about the Beast of Fame, and how antiheroes famed for being involved with a ghastly public circumstance are regarded with as much aplomb and hoohah as anyone who attained celebrity status by actually doing something of merit. I thought it my duty to attend and look him penetratingly in the eye.

Kato was the first person I talked to at the party. He was very attractive and pleasant, and urged my friend and me to enjoy the shrimp cocktail. Could this be the alleged coke-frosted couch monkey whose testimony was

invaluable to the loudest murder fiasco of the Universe?
He seemed well spoken and miscast.

The room was dotted over with fallen television icons
from the seventies, with big bronze putty heads full of
dark sticky eyes and teeth like salt cliffs. In an attack of
resonant Jungian referencing, I was reminded of the
three desiccated hag-Fates of myth who all wrangle over
one eye and one tooth ceaselessly and scream at each
other; anyone who doesn't have the Fame, particularly if
the Fame was yanked from them at one time, wants to be
in the same room with virtually anyone who does have it,
even if they got it for being connected to some heinous
atrocity. When a personality ceases to be famous, their
ego is a sun whose gravity collapses inward on itself and
becomes a black hole with an appetite for the limelight
which can never be sated. As voracious unpersonalities
sucked the angstroms off of Kato as he luminated weirdly
near the buffet table, you could hear their grated throats
hissing, "The EYE! The TOOTH! Give me the EYE!"
The famished need of such lost and bloodless personae
increases the glory of Kato, who will never be a pool
cleaner again and will never have a problem scoring
chicks. It may have looked like a pleasant hillside birthday party to those unconcerned with the event's status in
the religious cosmos, but my third eye witnessed nothing
but the chest-beating, keening, and clothes-rending of a
hapless clutch of Fame Junkies with deep, shuddering
joneses and ice sweats that were frightening and remark-
able to behold.

Why, you may ask, is widespread media attention such

a powerful and all-controlling force in human beings' per-
ception of other human beings? We were all terribly fond
of O. J. Simpson in the seventies for being part of the very
first man-to-man (not to mention interracial) tongue kissing ever on television (with Bill Murray in an *SNL* parody
of *Mandingo*); we now all think of him as a big greenish liar-
mouth festooned with terrible guilt and the oily broth of
the three-card-monte-esque jingoism spewed by Johnnie
Cochran. Still, if he were to appear suddenly in any restaurant, the nylons would melt off every woman in the room
and every man under the age of seventy would suck in his
gut and be stoned on the heightened mescaline-sensory
sensation of the air shimmering and having all the hair
stand up on their arms and back. He was a Great Man; now
he is a Great Big Scary Dangerous Creep, but they'd still
want to hang out with him. Those who scoff at the carrion-
eating Kato portrayed in the media would not deny themselves the privilege of sharing his shrimp cocktail. The
bloodbath connected with the fame of O.J. and Kato was
somehow whitewashed and rendered subordinate to the
fame itself, leaving them ultimately just as successful as if
they were the stars of a hit TV show, which, given the un-
precedented media coverage of the trial, they were. Fame,
after all, comes with no allegiance to ethics: it makes no
difference what disgrace one is famous for; celebrities are
made by quantities of fame, not qualities.

■

The nineties were a great decade for Atrocity. It seized
the limelight like a coke-angry Homecoming Queen.

A Massive Swelling

The union of man with nature was whacked another thirty degrees out of balance. Genetic-technology scientists grew human ears out of the backs of rats, and young children got stabbed and shot and smashed like flies and tossed off buildings every time you blinked, by people who had barely recovered from childhood themselves. The value of children, weirdly, seemed to drop in inverse proportion to the Dow Jones—as our stocks soared to record heights, the lives of kids somehow got shuffled down to the clearance rack.

■

America has drifted so low into the sweaty brine of moral atavism, it made me think that we're probably raising kids somehow wrong in America. Teenagers hate themselves, life is cheap, murder is simple. We can thank Hollywood's mythologizing of the Badass, in large part, for the fact that many disgruntled high-school students now feel that the most glamorous and exciting thing they can do is embrace the Dark Side, obtain assault rifles (with little difficulty), and go kill everybody in their homeroom. Teenagers seem to think it a fine thing to go to Hell these days. Mean and dumb patricidal "teen vampire cults" had the run of Kentucky for a while: "Shut UP, Mom! I am TOO a vampire! I was a DEMON in my LAST LIFE and I'm undead NOW so I don't HAVE to go to first-period English if I FUCKING DON'T WANT TO!" Perhaps the vampires are on to something, and parents who can't provide their children with limitless credit-card use and fresh hemoglobin should be bludgeoned to death, but somehow I don't think so. Naturally, everyone in the world has wanted to kill his or her parents or everyone in high school at some point, but never before has it seemed like an attractive or viable option, guaranteeing a type of toothsome infamy.

■

There is a tendency in Hollywood to glamorize everything we are supposed to be united against as civilized society, but the sad truth is, this glamour acts as a hypnotic pornography for those weak of mind and spirit. Hollywood has always gotten away with chilling hypocrisy: graphically showing a naked model getting raped and carved into a tiki sculpture, represented as a Bad Thing. But it generally sells as jerk-off material anyway. Violence is always very sexily portrayed on film. A few years ago I was watching the Q. Tarantino project *True Romance* in the theater. When Patricia Arquette finally wrangled the gun away and blasted the Bad Guy all over the walls, it was such a surging climax of a payoff I actually *left my body*, my soul shot out and *flew* for a moment, I was so gratified, and I thought I abhorred violence. I realized these ascendant moments represent a new form of American pornography: the cum shot of revenge.

■

Ultraviolence on film is usually wrapped around some thin, warped semblance of "honor": "Fuck you," says the movie's Nasty Evil Guy with the leather jacket and goatee. "No, fuck YOU" (RAT-TTA-TAT-A-TAT-ATA), says the

Badass Movie Hero in the leather jacket and goatee, toting
an automatic assault rifle, who kicks over the corpse, blows
the smoke off the barrel, and stalks off to kill anyone else
who annoys him. "Ha ha ha! YEAH!" say most of the dumb
fucks in the audience, for whom the film was made. "That
guy is cool!" The success of the Badass image seems to be
based in vicarious rage; Americans always seem to be on the
lookout for something that can vindicate a sudden, justified
outburst of kickboxing; they are always waiting with bated
breath, *Come on, fucker, try something,* just *itching* for some
dimwit in traffic, some random idiot bastard, to perpetrate
some injustice, no matter how minor, so they can justifiably
unleash a torrent of insane abuse; a rain of injury.

■

In the last few years, copycat murderers imitating *Natural
Born Killers* and *The Basketball Diaries* and the setting on
fire of New York token booths and countless other such
atrocious examples of "life imitating art" have become so
banal and commonplace that they barely register a blip on
the screen of American consciousness anymore—they're
unsurprising. Because of the frequency of such copycat
hate crimes, I find it especially scary and appalling that
Hollywood is still such a pushover for sexy films about
Nazis. Skinheads in films such as *American History X* and
Romper Stomper (an Aussie film that had wide American
distribution) are routinely presented as really macho, gorgeous, muscular gang boys with James Dean–ish appeal
and martyrlike political futility. Even if the script reads
like the worst, most didactic and plausibility-free eighth-

grade morality play ever told, the box office starts jingling with titillation, because *America loves to watch the Skins stomp the darkies*. I felt that *American History X* was, for all practical purposes, a serious tool of white-extremist, right-wing propaganda, with extremely careful, articulate arguments for racism and only the most cursory, banal token nod, at the very end, towards some vague sense of basic, nonmurderous rightness and humanitarianism. Ed Norton was absolutely luscious in that film, standing in the middle of a street, flexing his hairless, taut sculpture of an oily Aryan physique, glaring into the camera with his goatee and abdominals and swastika tattoos. When with a leonine roar Norton crushed the black car thief's skull on the curb with his boot in super-slo-mo, it was filmed with as much unctuous eroticism as when the bucket of icewater poured all over Jennifer Beals's tits in *Flashdance*.

That movie terrified the shit out of me—it terrified me that it even got *made*, that people in previews watched it and didn't see it as something as loathsome as a parade of liver-spotted brownshirts. But moviegoers ate it up, they loved it, just like everybody loves a film about a nice hooker, or copies of serial killer John Wayne Gacy's clown paintings.

■

Even the Christians are embracing the power of murderporn to get their point across. I was recently exposed to a religious-cum-educational videotape for "teens at risk" that has been distributed to various prisons and schools: *The Choice Is Yours—with David Berkowitz*. This video was a hardsell of harried, pro-life Christian propaganda built around an interview with America's original postal-worker-turned-psychopath, "Son of Sam" serial killer David Berkowitz, who has loudly undergone a vast born-again conversion while serving a life sentence without possibility of parole in the Sullivan Correctional Facility, a maximum-security prison.

The video paints a portrait of David Berkowitz as a nerdy fat kid and attributes his wholesale slide off the deep end to "drugs and drinking," "wanting to fit in," and "peer pressure" to be "cool." Berkowitz, who now refers to himself as "the Son of Hope," is a fat, ranty, used-car-salesman type of forty-seven-year-old Bronx guy, who thumbs obsessively through a red plastic Bible and pro-claims that he was "a real jerk" back during his murder spree in the mid-seventies, when at the behest of Sam, his neighbor's black Labrador retriever, he would find young couples making out in cars and girls with long, brown hair and shoot them in the face.

What I couldn't stop thinking about was, What kind of Christian organization would stoop to *using the celebrity of a serial killer to promote teen interest in Christianity?* Roll over, Jesus.

I felt the same horror when I read about Doreen Lioy, the woman who married Richard "Night Stalker" Ramirez. One can barely imagine the life a woman must have led that would make an option such as marrying a Satan-worshiping death-row murderer/rapist a Joyous Event.

One can only assume that Ms. Lioy, for vainglorious reasons, wanted to attach the press-aggrandized Night Stalker Mystique to herself, and she probably got it. She was probably treated very differently at the neighborhood Arby's when she glared ominously at the waitstaff through her sienna-tinted lenses; her hatred suddenly had some celebrity *weight*. As opposed to being written off as another bitter single woman with damaged hair and too much makeup in a black corduroy country-western jacket, she was finally regarded in her community as some sort of tacit semithreat. The locals now treat her with the reverence that Fear inspires. She is undoubtedly proud to wield this aura of Danger-by-Marriage, and will exercise it at every possible opportunity. Formerly a powerless and invisible person, she now causes a discomfort in others that very nearly *smells like animal respect*. Having married a famous murderer, she now feels somehow "safe."

■

There is a prophetic scene in the wonderful Paddy Chayefsky movie *Network* (a film outrageous enough to be funny in the seventies) that perfectly articulates America's love for extreme displays of hatred. Faye Dunaway's character, Diana Christensen, the ambitious television executive, suggests to her development team that their fall season lineup include suicides, Mafia executions, and terrorist bombings: "The American people are turning sullen. They've been clobbered on all sides by Vietnam, Watergate, the Inflation, the Depression, they've turned off, shot up and fucked themselves limp and nothing helps. . . . The American people WANT someone to articulate their rage for them." This is particularly poignant when one takes into account the recent emergence (not to mention astonishing popularity) of shows like *Real Life Home Videos of Bloody Disasters and Pets Who Hate*. Mainstream media veering towards exploitation and tabloid is nothing new . . . it's the new LEVEL of it that's alarming.

Joey Buttafuoco, neckless reamer of As Seen on TV psychoteen-convict Amy Fisher, made the scene for a few years at the Right Parties with his bullet-warped wife. John Wayne Bobbitt, ex-castrato, made a career out of dropping his panties and familiarizing the world with his evil reanimated knob. Jeff Gillooly showed himself to be one of the most nauseatingly hateful cads in tabloid history when he released his unretouched animal-rump wedding night with violent ice-whore/eyesore Tonya Harding. Monica Lewinsky, overweight Presidential blow-jobbist, was easily the most popular person at the 1999 Oscar parties immediately following the scandal. Any of these people are treated with as much, if not more, of the glittery nervousness in elevators that nonfamous people reserve for the likes of real stars. In fact, most nonfamous people would be MORE excited seeing someone from the aforementioned antihero list than they would be seeing someone really interesting, like Noam Chomsky or Yo-Yo Ma. This kind of nonsensical and value-slashed attitude must stop immediately. There are far too many rewards to be reaped in this society for shamelessly sporting one's befouled ethical pants around the ankles.

■

As Martin Luther King once said, a man should be judged not by the color of his skin, but by the content of his character. Dr. King's sentiment should go duly noted when the skin happens to be phosphorescent and blue from flash cubes. Let us not worship these people, for it is like bowing down to a two-headed calf: unholy and weird.

PART FOUR

ORCHESTRA TICKETS TO GRIEF

CHAPTER 14

A Few Short Words on the Literary Life

*E*very day, bookwise, at least, I am aware of clumpy, dribbling blockbuster sensations like *The Bridges of Madison County* or *Chicken Soup for the Teenage Soul* or *Memoirs of a Geisha* and I feel as if one of those painful African parasite-worms has lodged in one of my arteries and grown miles in length through my entire nervous system and is now being wound out of my eye inch by inch on a wooden spool.

■

Art isn't fair. Henry Miller lived in a large, wet ashtray for most of his adult life, crippled by open syphilis lesions and earsplitting shame. Nathanael West, a writer who really counts, couldn't get noticed by the literary community in his time if he ran through one of their luncheons wearing nothing but small circular burn marks and being chased by a pack of blood-and-chalk-spattered aborigines.

•

I went through mammoth, multiple flaming-hoop procedures to get a deal to write this book. It was weird and hard and demoralizing, because these days, just being an award-winning writer for twelve years doesn't necessarily mean you're capable of writing a book. These days, even the most loyal cult readership can't turn the money heads in publishing land. What you really need to do to get a book deal these days is: either have your own TV show, have a son or daughter with his/her own TV show, win an Olympic medal, or fuck murderers.

There are exceptions, of course. If you happen to be a female sex worker, you can get a six-figure book deal, no problem; or if you're writing exclusively about sex you can generally cash in like a discount crack outlet. Or you can be in a sexually themed coffee-table book—there are a couple of girls who I know who became successful in that field. One is a stripper who is now famous for being a Satanist who drinks blood, who is in a coffee-table photo book drooling blood all over her tits. The other one is a stripper who is now famous for being in a different popular photo book doggie-style with a lit candle sticking out of her ass. They're doing very well.

There have been rashes of TV/popular personalities targeted by the book world for contributions to the best-seller rack: great minds of our generation such as Jenny McCarthy, O. J. Simpson concubine Paula Barbieri, Fran Drescher, and several others, including the mom of Ellen DeGeneres. Drescher, in this lineup, is practically Dorothy Parker. A tragic heroine like little Ekaterina Gordeeva with her "I lost my husband but still I skate onwards" book is practically Eleanor Roosevelt.

Here are several ideas for celebrity books that I'd love to be in on, to be ghostwritten by myself, so if you are any of these celebrities, please contact me through my publisher ($$$!):

1. *The Great Big Book of Eating Disorder Confessions*, Dominique Moceanu, editor
2. *What JonBenet Would Have Said: Projected Speculations of a Young Personality*
3. Brandy/Moesha: *The Two Phat Decades of My Life* and
4. Madonna: *Middle-Aged SEX After Childbirth* (mostly David LaChapelle photos)

Books like these have given would-be authors the wrong idea. They think that they should be able to wank out a depraved memoir at the age of twenty-five and get a $150,000 advance and spend it all getting drunk at the Lapin Agile. I say a serious writer should be pounding out big ugly stacks of worthless prattle for nothing but his/her own self-humiliation. For nothing but the excesses of solitude, masturbation, and lower back pain. Otherwise, they should forget about writing and start working at Grand Auto and clocking $7.50 an hour.

■

To aspiring writers, I say this:

Don't write four angry poems and some tea-stained short stories about your vagina and expect them to rain you with lucre and laurels. You want a trophy, go learn how to bowl. If you want to write, God help you.

CHAPTER 15

Mein Überkampf:
The Unfair Distributions
of Cash and Joy in the World

In the time of hedonist fascism, nobody dares scream or judge what is so pathetically suspended in mid-air, which is life itself. . . . Meaning that if you aren't mad, you're crazy—we are being eaten body and soul and no one is fighting. In fact, practically no one sees it, but if you listen to the poets you will hear, and vomit up your rage.

—LESTER BANGS

A few years ago, I had one of those New Age dreams where I was hovering bodiless out in the middle of space, staring down at the earth, surrounded by a bunch of Older and Wiser invisible beings who talked to me in my head. I noticed that the earth was surrounded by these things that looked like enormous, greasy black snakes with heads huge and round like opium poppies. They seemed to be strangling the atmosphere of the little blue planet. "What are the snake things?" I asked. "Greed," the Older/Wiser/Spiritually Important voices said. I noticed that nearly the whole planet was coiled around with these writhing snakes like fisted arms—only little puddles of ocean peeked through, and a couple of polar caps.

The Lakota tribe felt that terrible things would happen if you impeded the divine flow of wealth; if the lucky in the tribe weren't super-generous and didn't give away whole-heartedly everything that they valued the most, disaster would occur. A stoppage in the flow of gifts was regarded with the same alarm as a stoppage in the flow of blood.

•

I have long been of the opinion that people with absurd amounts of money need to be periodically retrained to appreciate it. Anybody who makes seven digits a year should be annually required to go on grueling Outward Bound–type expeditions for a couple of months and forced to erect lean-tos and eat bark to survive. Only fifty thousand years ago, that's what we all did, and we were happy and considered ourselves lucky. Now a handful of people have billions of dollars, while whole nations of people shrivel and wheeze and die in the dust because they can't afford drinking water, and this is somehow considered OK.

What do you do with a spare billion dollars? Does anybody really have any fucking idea? Have your own air

A Massive Swelling

force? Buy the presidency, like fiendish elf Ross Perot almost did? The Sultan of Brunei hires lots of beautiful women to hang out on his island, to play tennis and ride bareback and play shuffleboard in thongs for thirty thousand dollars a week. I suppose you could have scientists coat all of your internal organs with Teflon, and have some kind of Swiss-made diamond-encrusted oyster-perpetual liver installed that you could never destroy through unrestrained alcoholism. A bionic eye might be nice, or maybe a state-of-the-art, built-in opposite sex part, so you can fuck yourself.

■

GOING BROKE ON 33 MILLION A YEAR, barked *People* magazine a while ago, citing the glittering bankrupt: M. C. Hammer in his Hammertime had to build his own Epcot Center of a home, with bathtubs big enough for eight and solid-gold quarterhorses; Kim Basinger's head was so large, it needed its own town; Shannen Doherty was living the life of a Middle Eastern armaments dealer until her checks stopped working. Burt Reynolds's insatiable need for human hair outspent several public schools in the last ten years. The list goes on and on. Now things have changed. Now, I guess, they need to play the accordion at bus stations and/or give hand jobs behind the Laundromat to survive. Chapter 11 is not for the proud, but for Christ's sake, nobody NEEDS a couple dozen miles of Georgia. You don't have to live like some kind of Colombian drug godfather to have a good time.

■

It is clear that superrich people should be punished, because they didn't get where they are today without having eaten a live human baby at some point in their career, or put their dick in somebody's grandma's earhole. Nobody makes that much money by being Christlike and giving. The Forbes 500 is full of misanthropic scallywags who desperately need a kick in the pants. Pale computer larvae like Gates and Dell and Bezos need to join the Marine Reserves and do calisthenics in the sun with rifles a couple times a month, and build free drug-rehab centers for those who have lived for nothing but perverse self-indulgence.

Warren Buffett needs to have his head shaved and be forced to be a waterboy for the Pittsburgh Steelers several times a year. The Mars choco-bar family ought to be made personally responsible for the nutrition and good mouth-feel of all inner-city school lunch programs. The Walton Wal-Mart family should give free diapers to any family with an income less than twenty thousand dollars a year. Prince Alwaleed Bin Talal Alsaud of Saudi Arabia ought to do something nice for those stepped-on Middle Eastern ladies. He ought to build them all a nice lesbian bathhouse. Then maybe they can have some fun. Why doesn't Phil Knight of Nike buy Africa, and declare it some kind of duchy in which internecine war factions are forced to play soccer to air their grievances?

■

A MASSIVE SWELLING

When people get rich, many also get puzzlingly cheap. Successful New York career women, according to a recent article in *The New York Times*, can't even find love anymore, because they put so much importance on dating men that are more financially successful than they are, and there aren't very many of those. What few eligible superrich guys there are have their time taken up by being immature louts and obsessively fumping twenty-two-year-old models. Why? Nowadays, since everything famous is Holy, none of the old rules apply. Money *can* buy you anything, anything you want—love, talent, beauty, credibility, spirituality, whatever. The world is on the auction block, baby; all you need is the clams.

■

There's a piece of the "True Cross" in a triptych in the J. P. Morgan Library, which the old sot chucked in his shopping basket at one point along with one of his three Gutenberg Bibles. One Gutenberg Bible, OK. Three?! Nobody, not even a library, needs three Gutenberg Bibles. It is like having three Barbra Streisands; but *Fuck it,* said old J.P., I *want* them, they're mine, mine, mine. Let the winos boil their cats in the Bowery. My fellow man can kiss my rich financier ass. I am the Sun King.

■

Ironically, rich people will give money for a good cause as long as it guarantees them a brush with celebrity.

I went to Christie's, the famed auction house, to watch Eric Clapton's guitars be auctioned off. The Clapton auction was something of a sociological masterpiece. Here you had Clapton, a rock dinosaur who had long since used up all of his sexy points in the Universe but could still cough out a top movie sound track every now and then. He's got a little rehab center in Antigua, so to show his commitment to "free treatment" for his drug-addict brethren (although it was unclear how to apply for the free detox: What kind of drug addicts did we need to be? Musical drug addicts? *Antiguan* drug addicts? "Consult our Web site," said the center's front desk when we called. Ahhh, we realized: hopeless addicts with *Web* access), Clapton auctions off one hundred guitars, two vintage amplifiers, and three Gianni Versace guitar straps, which looked like they could have been latter-day fat Elvis's Las Vegas bugle-bead judo belts, with just a skosh of Native American.

What was being auctioned off, essentially, were relics of the True Cross—i.e., the guitars that Eric played when Eric was at his best, the Guitar God, the Clapton who wrote and performed the seminal "Layla." It was better that today's Clapton wasn't actually present for the auction, being all old and VH1 and adult contemporary and full of sober crotchetiness in a black dinner jacket; it made all of the necrophiliac fan-worship that much more so: there was a time in the seventies when Clapton was a horse fiend, and burnt by the eye of God and perceived as brilliant, and ironically, it was this dead, smack-inspired Clapton that the auction people were pouring money over, much in the way the prices will triple for a dead painter.

A Massive Swelling

The room at Christie's was packed to bursting with middle-aged rich people full of adolescent preconcert adrenaline. Most of the buyers seemed to be fat old rock-'n'-rollers, gray-haired balding boys with ponytails in Hawaiian shirts and prescription sunglasses. There were a lot of mealy, concave business guys, and some perplexing older women in Prada dresses with ancient green tattoos. Standing to the side was a row of beautiful boys and girls in crisp little jackets, manning the telephones for the anonymous Big Money boys out to own a piece of the Clap. Everyone caught the fever the second the bidding started for the first lot, and the famous-guitar prices immediately shot into the moaning, head-shaking stratosphere.

When the "Layla" guitar, the last lot on the auction block, turned around in the little carousel, and "Layla" started blasting over the loudspeakers, the room flipped into the latent chaos it had been politely suppressing all day. People stood up and howled. Everyone took flash pictures. People began salaaming the stage, bowing to the old guitar, with the varnish worn off the frets from Clapton wizardry. Others began demurely headbanging. They started the bids at $200K. Chills ran up my legs. When the bids ended at $450K, we all were nauseated and euphoric: the post-obscene-splurge thrill of guilty spending and dirtiness coursed through us all like a contact high on the dance floor. Oooh, I realized, this is how rich people party.

The whole thing was too interesting: a mass psychosis, an escalating of value for objects that had been used by famous hands, an escalation that informed and invented itself every time the bid jumped another 10K; the roomful of people realized that they were turning up the value on pop-cultural objects forever; they were deciding what famous icons were worth, what their love and memories of these icons were worth, and praying to them in the only profound way it seems Americans know how to pray anymore, which is with money.

After the auction, the pinkly elated checkwriters could be found sitting in the carpeted corridors with their redeemed lots, strumming their own rusty, thumb-screwed renditions of Subcommandante Clapton's repertoire, shrug-faced and apologetic for the TV cameras, already rubbing the magical fingerprints off the rosewood with their sweaty, rich little mitts.

■

The thing that gets me is that the people with all the cash advantages are also the people who seem to be having the most fun in the world. This is not what Hollywood tells us in films, but it is what celebrity culture shows us by example. Movies continually patronize us with the idea that the Common Man with his Common Life is the most hallowed and joyous thing in the world; yet neither a single celebrity motherfucker nor anyone else in the world would ever, ever, ever give up a single moment of prancing in a Versace ballgown down the red-carpeted paparazzi gauntlet in order to volunteer at the DMV or sell towels at Bullock's. Why would they? Their life is a nonstop, star-spangled kick in the pants.

A Massive Swelling

Case in point: Supermodel Shalom Harlow lived in my old New York neighborhood, with her equally inhumanly pretty boyfriend, and the problem with them was, they appeared to be having an absolutely wonderful life.

She is one of the highest-paid people in the world. God knows who he is, but they undoubtedly met at some gala fashion show in some old garden palace in Firenze, where she was draped in the Gaudí courtyard against a twilit fig tree with morning glories twisted into her bangs, wearing nothing but a sheer organza tube slip and a $75,000 tangle of rare orange pearls, drinking a Dom Pérignon Bellini out of a Tang dynasty fingerbowl. He was probably looking for the ivory-tipped dart he had rashly shot out of an original Zulu blowgun that was only borrowed and supposed to be a prop, and he found it sticking suggestively in the treetrunk's crotch about an inch and a half over her sleek, minky ocean of brunet curls, and huge blue eyes met huger blue eyes and they spoke in some kind of inaudible, spiritual free-prose and recognized that physical perfection and love and wealth had all instantaneously achieved some obscene, whirling celestial synthesis between them, and that they were the Original Man and Original Woman restored to power in Eden in the late twentieth century.

They were always clutching each other and giggling and kissing deeply but politely in the supermarket and whispering important little secrets to each other, dressed down exactly alike in their sealed, hermetic world, and everyone else who came within twenty feet of them looked like criminally obese shrub trolls, wretched from cosmic justice's foiling of their own selfish and foul-minded plans.

There goes the .0000000009 percent, I would say from the depths of my depressing physical and spiritual lack, when I saw Shalom and her Man. All the looks, all the cash, and all the fun, apparently. Glad somebody's having everything all at once. I just wish everything was a little more evenly distributed. It's so hard to watch.

Around that same time, the other 99.9999999991 percent was mourning the death of the Woolworth's drug and discount stores, while two brand-new Dolce & Gabbanas opened in New York, with ten-foot photomurals of Shalom and her physiological equivalent in the windows, sporting $2,000 plastic raincoats and $130 stocking caps.

On one of the final days of Woolworth's, I too was shopping with the Great Unwashed at the senile five-and-dime, where you could once find anything from lawnmower cozies to oil lamps shaped like golden owls to Barbie windmills, and top it all off with a ninety-nine-cent chili dog and an Orange Julius. By the time I got there, the shelves were a savaged carcass with all of the packaging entrails gored and exposed; nobody was bothering to restack or rewrap anything. The store was an old, obsolete creature that had already died; its custodians would never again bother to clip on its mock necktie or help its arthritic hands open a can of vienna sausages or mix up its home permanent kit again. Woolworth's was long past those modest vanities, and now the carrion shoppers were performing their entropic role.

A Massive Swelling

When I was standing in line with a pair of stockings and a couple of picture frames, I saw who the Woolworth's family was: all the jittery, blotchy, innocent elderly people on terrifically constricted budgets, buying up the last new washcloths they'd ever use; young black women buying armloads of normally prohibitively priced baby accessories; and hard young professional $16,000/yr. temp chicks with their plastic baskets filled with discounted cosmetics—probably the same frustrated young women who ballpointed the goatee and round glasses on the cosmetic-display photo of Shalom Harlow, staring winsomely out at Woolworth's shoppers through her glossy cardboard window from an empyreal galaxy far, far away. The poor neighborhood old folks would undoubtedly really miss their Woolworth's, where they could always buy their Kleenex pocket packs and Suave hand lotion, and treat themselves to a nice grilled American-cheese sandwich and Carnation ice milk for 10 percent off every Thursday. There was a lot more need in New York for the Woolworth's, but New York thinks old people are gross and is probably trying to get rid of them. Eeeu! Get away, Grampa, you're all, like, OLD! New York fancies itself a young and hip and beautiful city. The seniors should all be shipped by train to Arizona and kept on painkillers in some sprawling adobe death camp.

■

I was flying back to the United States from Jakarta, and I was listening to some obnoxious young woman, apparently an ad executive, talking to a couple of older guys who were apparently also ad executives. Like me, she was on her way back from superimpoverished Indonesia.

"So I had this pair of shoes," she was saying in the hyperanimated, entitled-to-your-rapt-attention way that spoiled little girls who get older always have, "and let me tell you, they smelled *so bad,* I decided to leave them behind! So I'm taking these shoes out of my bag near this village and these people started *running* up to me and saying 'Nike American! Nike American!' and offering me trades! So I was like, 'Sure, I'll take that sarong—I'll take that wall clock—I'll take that and that!'" She began laughing, and the two older men started laughing with her.

"This woman finally tried my shoes on," she continued, "and I kid you not, she started to walk to work in them and she was *crying.* Tears—I'm not kidding you—were rolling down her face."

"Nike American!" said one of the men as an explanation—subtext: Best Shoes in the world! Why, I'd cry too; who wouldn't?

"Yep! The real McCoy!" said the girl.

The whole exchange turned me so emotionally sideways, I wanted to hit both of them with a nine-iron until they didn't move anymore. I really go crazy with hatred when the overprivileged act like they are the only three-dimensional entities in the world and everyone else is an amusing finger puppet, doing some crazy backward nigger dance for their enjoyment.

According to Michael Moore's great lefty diatribe *Downsize This,* 36 percent of all retail Nikes are made in

Indonesia, by young women who work fifty hours a week for a starting rate of two dollars a day, a wage they can't live on. It would take most Indonesian villagers around two months to earn a pair of Nikes, and that's if they didn't spend any money eating or living. Nike may have suffered a little stockwise when this fact came out, but not enough to seriously dent the Nike superstructure or cause them to Repent. The 250 million dollars that Nike spent on advertising in 1994 has successfully brainwashed all world ghettos, even the very people that Nike itself is keeping below the poverty line: Nikes are the magic shoes, the real McCoy; they can make you jump so high you can catch a glimpse of that world on luminous billboards and the international power-glow of MTV. Michael Jordan and Tiger Woods can buy as much of Georgia as they want to, while one-third of all the other black males in America are in jail; many of them are then forced to stitch sportswear for two dollars a day. Nike American. Show your love for Michael Jordan, own a true piece of the hero, share the diamond-studded frame with the face of God.

■

Perhaps local unions should be established to safeguard the fair distribution of worldly pleasure. The fact is, not all men are created equal and not all worldly goods are delivered equally. The pyramid with the eyeball on the dollar bill is an allegory for capitalism and may as well be an allegory for fame: all is labor and darkness for the bricks at the wide bottom, but at the rarefied tippy-top, everything is radiant, cognizant, and blinding. The super-rich are smart enough to perch atop everybody else's missing Stuff, and celebrities are overblown enough to absorb everybody else's missing love and attention. Both groups have a deeply perverted sense of overentitlement. There is a passage from Tom Wolfe's *Electric Kool-Aid Acid Test* where Ken Kesey writes of a bad acid trip: "*'I'm ME!... That's the cry of the ego ... ME! ME! ME! ME!... and that's why wars get fought ... ego ... because enough people want to scream Pay attention to ME....'*"

Hollywood is where an elite few MEs get recognized at the expense of everyone else's. This gross imbalance in human attention has resulted in a slow but profound brainwashing—now everyone feels that their ME needs to be hugely recognized or their ME doesn't quite exist, and they suffer like brick-eating dingoes. *Even your parents will love you more if you're rich and famous,* sayeth our corrupted DNA. To live with anything else is to live with a haunting degree of failure. Only when we are rich and famous can we truly relax.

▪

Celebrity is a virulent killer of fundamental human values, and unless Southern California goes up in a shiny mushroom cloud on Judgment Day, the only way to control it is to quit believing in it. Most sophisticated people don't think they do believe in Fame, but they do, in a deep, fearful, insidious way. When you *really stop* believing in the sexual comeliness of the ninety-eight-pound blonde with the saline D-cups, in the commercial earnestness of young athletes or the infantile cuteness of Goldie Hawn; when you rub the maribou from Madonna's bra out of your eyes and are no longer dazzled by Schwarzenegger's Hummer or Liberace's rhinestoned piano, the Emperor is a fat, naked freak and it all looks sick and ridiculous.

We need to stop accepting as the height of culture whatever we see on the shiniest cardboard displays, and stop letting Viacom dictate culture. We need to stop believing that anything "alternative" is "hip." We must seek out obscure artsy anomalies from all over the world that appeal to us for weird, twingey, unknown reasons. We must cease to find glamour in the mondo-expensivo Eurofag Gucci footwear camps, just because magazines tell us they're glamorous. We must learn to be more impressed by the dignified, esoteric details in other, boring and thoughtful walks of life. We must stop believing that famous people are sexier and better and more beautiful and interesting than other people. They're not. They're just like other human beings, only *advertised*, massively, into major leading brands, like dog food or shaving cream.

■

Stop pathetically believing that you deserve Fame or Fame deserves you. It's yucky, and it's only making you miserable, so stop.

CHAPTER 16

A Composer, a Director, a Writer, the Greatest Band in the World, 3 Movies, 2 Surfers

1. Stevie Wonder
2. Akira Kurosawa
3. Lester Bangs
4. Tenacious D
5. *A Thousand Clowns*
6. *Network*
7. *The Philadelphia Story*
8. Cory and Shea Lopez

Acknowledgments

The author would like to express boundless gratitude to David Talbot and Gary Kamiya, for letting me grow up on their payroll, and for their outstanding guidance and support. This book would not be a book if it had not been purchased by the glamorous Courtney Hodell, and subsequently edited into coherence by the sparkling and invaluable Molly Stern.

I thank my hilarious and wonderful honcho, Kent; my family, and my new family in Arizona; and all of my great friends who have put up with my fretful daytime phone calls over the years, especially Mo and Charity.

Alafia.